GA 328

THE SOCIAL QUESTION

by

RUDOLF STEINER

A Series of Six Lectures by Rudolf Steiner
given at Zurich, 3 February through 8 March 1919

Schmidt Numbers:
3649, 3651, 3655, 3657, 3664, 3671

Translation and Artwork by Hanna von Maltitz

This translation is provided through a grant from the
Basil Gibaud Memorial Trust

The e.Lib, Inc.
in cooperation with
The Rudolf Steiner Archive & e.Lib
Fremont, Michigan, USA

First English Edition 2017

Rudolf Steiner Archive & e.Lib
Fremont, Michigan, USA

These lectures are a translation from the German edition *Die soziale Frage*, (Bn/GA Number 328 in the Bibliographical Survey, 1961), published by the Rudolf Steiner-Nachlassverwaltung, Dornach, Switzerland, 1977. They are published as transcripts unrevised by the lecturer. This First English edition was translated by Hanna von Maltitz, and was edited by James D. Stewart, e.Librarian at the Rudolf Steiner Archive & e.Lib.

Illustrations and artwork were created by Hanna von Maltitz. Thanks to the Basil Gibaud Memorial Trust, this translation has been made available.

ISBN: 978-1-948302-00-5 (paperback)
978-1-948302-01-2 (eBook)

Published in the United States of America

PUBLISHER'S NOTE

In his autobiography, *The Course of My Life* (chapter 35 and chapter 36), Rudolf Steiner speaks as follows concerning the character of this privately printed matter:

"The contents of this printed matter were intended as oral communications and not for print ...

"Nothing has ever been said that was not the purest result of Anthroposophy as it developed ... Whoever reads this privately printed matter can take it in the fullest sense as that which Anthroposophy has to say. Therefore, it was possible, and moreover without misgivings ... to depart from the accepted custom of circulating these publications only among the membership. But it will have to be remembered that faulty passages occur in the transcripts, which I myself did not revise.

"The right to form a judgment on the content of such privately printed matter can be admitted only in the case of one who has acquired the requisite preliminary knowledge. And in respect of all these publications, this is, at the very least, the knowledge of man and of the cosmos in so far as it is presented in Anthroposophy, and of what is to be found as 'anthroposophical history' in the communications from the spiritual world."

TRANSLATOR'S NOTE

Dear Reader, I wish you could experience the content of these lectures as a listener, for that was the way in which they were presented. Please imagine Rudolf Steiner speaking to you in these lectures rather than finding hiccups in some of his long sentences. Difficulties abound for a translator in finding just one pesky word to convey the richness of German composite words, but trying to offer the reader a string of alternate words which might fit, could be utterly confusing. One particular term needs some explanation.

The lectures deal with the "Proletariat". Dictionaries translate this word as the *common worker, bourgeoisie, the working-class people, the labour class, the lower classes, the masses, the plebeians*, and so on. The use of the word "Proletarian" started rising in the 1900 and peaked at around 1930 and again 1980. I leave it up to you to make the switch in your mind when you come across this word, to one of your choice.

The same can be done for "bourgeoisie", a word Rudolf Steiner uses at times and which fits the same formula as above. Yet it may extend to refer to *folk*, to *the general public*, and so on. A reference to "class" distinction is avoided.

In the second lecture Rudolf Steiner suggests that the first four lectures are taken as a unit, and not be judged as single statements. The final two lectures could likewise form a unit because they were given as Public Lectures, in other words they were not limited to members of the Anthroposophical Society. These two lectures take on quite a different tone and a brave front and it is well worth your perseverance to reach the end.

HANNA VON MALTITZ.
November 2017.

CONTENTS

SUMMARIES OF LECTURES

Lecture 1: Zurich, 3 February 1919

The Social Question: "The true form."

The actual form of the social question understood out of life's necessities at present, on the basis of scientific spiritual research unannounced in the social needs of the present. Regarding the origin of the proletarian movement. The problem with cause and effect. The proletarian class distinction in relation to human consciousness. The ideological character of science, art and religion for the proletariat. Contradictions in the proletarian movement. Towards a Threefold Social Order.

Lecture 2: Zurich, 5 February 1919

The Social Question: "More on the Social Question."

A comparison between the attempts at solving the social question based on life's realities and the necessity for a scientific spiritual concept of life as a social organism. Criticism of analogy. Structural features of the Threefold Social organism. Inherent laws in spiritual, legal, and economic life. Arguments against the centralisation of social functional areas. The meaning of freedom, equality and brotherhood for the social organism. Perspectives for social reform.

Lecture 3: Zurich, 10 February 1919

The Social Question: "Fanaticism versus a real conception of life in social thinking and willing."

Extremism vs a real view of life in social thinking and willing. The being and meaning of the proletarian view of life during the evolution of mankind. The meaning of a spiritual scientific world view for the establishment of a social reality. Social utopia and fanaticism. Criticism for state monopoly in spiritual and cultural life. Regarding the value of human labour – criticism of Karl Marx.

Lecture 4: Zurich, 12 February 1919

The Social Question: "The Evolution of Social Thinking and Social Willing and life's circumstances."

The development of social thinking and will and life's circumstances for present humanity and their influences of individual behaviour. Two streams in social thinking and social feeling. Illusion of cause-and-effect running in a straight line in social developments. Instinctive feelings and modern individual consciousness. Regarding national economic thoughts of physiocrats (value based on land and labour). The relationship between legal and economic life. The tasks of legality. Thoughts towards the main social law. Private right and criminal law as components of spiritual life. Present day question from the point of view of Threefoldness.

Lecture 5: Zurich, 25 February 1919 (Public Lecture)

The Social Question: "Student lecture on Social Willing."

Public lecture on social will as forming the basis of a new scientific order. Regarding superstitious abstraction from which something lively can be formed. Community building. The question of human dignity in modern thinking. Spirituality regarded as an ideology, a mirror of materialistic reality. Denationalization as a guiding force of social change. Regarding the nature of human labour and the necessity of revealing its character. Schooling pupils in social will. Freedom, Equality and Brotherhood. Social need and social reality.

Lecture 6: Zurich, 8 March 1919 (Public Lecture)

The Social Question: "What significance does work have for the modern proletarians?"

The meaning of modern civilization for evolution. The split brought about through modernism. Results of education for the Proletariat. Human dignity in the workplace. Capitalism. Labour sold as Goods. The function of the state from the perspective of the ruling classes. The State as a Cooperative. The definition of human labour in a healthy social organism. Science and the working classes. The economic vs legal state. The state's dominance over cultural and economic life. The principle of association as a basis for a contemporary economic system. Money. The necessity for a Threefold Social Organism. Closing words after the discussion. Being one with the common workers.

ON-LINE ACTIVITIES

Research GA 328 Editions On-line

www.rsarchive.org/Lectures/GA328/

Side-by-Side Compare Editions

www.rsarchive.org/Lectures/GA328/Compare/index.php

Search this Edition

wn.rsarchive.org/Lectures/GA328/English/eLib2017/dosearch.html

Research this Edition

wn.rsarchive.org/Lectures/GA328/English/eLib2017/index.html

THE TRUE FORM OF THE SOCIAL QUESTION

Lecture 1

by Rudolf Steiner

given at Zurich, 3 February 1919

wn.rsarchive.org/Lectures/GA328/English/eLib2017/19190203p01.html

The concept contained in the words "social question" is something which thinking humanity has been occupied with for decades, occupied because this question has not only become urgent for the evolution of humanity, but it has become a burning question. In particular, one may say that the terrible war catastrophe which has broken over mankind during recent years has thrown its dark light on the social question in particular and its correlation to humanity's mobility in the immediate present.

As I wish to place the social enigma within the totality of history of more recent times I need to address in my upcoming lectures various things which are connected to the cause and course of the terrible catastrophe of war. In these introductory explorations, I only need to point out how, already at the war's starting point, it is clear how the social question works itself into every emotion of fear, clearly seen in those present at the beginning of the war. Certainly, a lot would have changed in 1914 when those who had encountered difficult decisions here or there, would no longer have stood under the fear of the question: 'What will happen if the social movement becomes increasingly pertinent?' Much which has crystallized out of this so-called war has sprung out of fear on the one hand and under complete misunderstanding of some leading personalities regarding the social question, on the other. Things would have developed in a different way if this fear and misunderstanding were not there. Then again, in the course of the war we see how personalities, who are active within the social movement, call for hope in themselves and others to activate the actual possibility towards restoring balance in the disharmony which has entered in such a shocking way into people's lives. Now, because these tragic events have infiltrated in a type of crisis, we see specific results have been left in the conquered countries: the most urgent necessity to take a stand towards the social question and to intervene in the social demands appearing in the history of this time.

Out of all of this, a thinking person viewing life at present, who wants to become familiar with present day habits, can gather how something appears in the social question which all members of humanity have been occupied with for an extremely long time. Just at this moment when, as we said, solutions to the social question are promoted in these conquered countries, something like tragedy is stored in the largest part of civilised humanity.

By looking at the spiritual efforts, at literature and anything similar which for many decades have appeared within meetings and in discussions with the intention of relating them to the social question, it appears as an immense amount of human labour in the minds of mankind. Never before has the social question been approached with such liveliness as today. Today the social demands are apparent in life itself. Despite all efforts, penetrating thoughts, despite the best will being shown in the last decades which have been instilled in capabilities, it was still insufficient to deal with the social question as it comes to the fore in its true form today when placed before the life of the human soul. Something unbelievably tragic is stored against the efforts of present day humanity. Something on which humanity has been preparing itself for such a long time, now met only those who one would like to believe had authority, but for which they were apparently quite unprepared.

For those who weren't occupied with the social question from the viewpoint of theoretical science, nor out of mere notions and not from one sided party views in the last decades, those would have discovered that the most powerful contradictions of life in just these areas always come to light. Perhaps the following is one of the most obvious contradictions in the areas of social life which has come forward. Much has been heard in discussion, much can be read by people whose lives are orientated towards the modern social movement. When within the midst of a discussion, standing within the will of a modern workforce itself one always has the feeling: Yes, here various things are discussed regarding many questions and various life forces. There is an attempt to give one or the other impulse a direction. However, in what one could call social will is something completely different to what is spoken about. Regarding any kind of event in life, no can one come to a clearer feeling than this: a more or less greater role is played by the subconscious, undeclared elements than what comes to the fore through apparently clear concepts delivered in a sober discussion. Here is the point where one can find the connection and not doubt the attempt in approaching the social question from a specific point of view.

Here in Zurich and in other Swiss towns I have often spoken about the question of spiritual science. From the standpoint of spiritual scientific research, I have also approached the social question for decades. If you hear about people who consider themselves practical you can certainly doubt that a convincing result will solve some relevant question out of simple spiritual research. Only contradiction, which I have pointed out in the striving within social life, drives away this doubt. One sees how important personalities within the social movement smile when the argument turns to people's desire to find a solution for the social question out of this or that spiritual effort; they smile because for them it is an ideology, a grey theory. Out of thoughts, out of mere spiritual life, so they think, nothing can be attributed towards the burning social question of the present. However, if you look more closely then it becomes obvious how the actual nerve, the actual foundation for the modern-day proletarian movement does not lie in what they are talking about, but it lies in their thoughts.

The modern proletarian movement is, perhaps like no other similar movement in the world — when one looks more closely it strikes you in the most imminent way — a movement born out of thoughts. This I don't say purely out of consideration. If I'm permitted to add a personal remark it would be this: For years I have taught in an educational school among the most varied branches of proletarian workers. I learnt to know what lives and strives in the souls of the modern proletarian worker. From this I came to recognise what lived in the labour unions in the most varied occupations and range of professions. Thus, not only from the point of view of theoretic consideration like in a clever play of words do I want to express it, but as the result of a real experience in life. Whosoever — this is so seldom the case in leading intellectuals — has learnt to know the modern worker's movement, where it is carried by the workers, will know what a wonderful phenomenon this is, how a certain direction of thought, a certain stream of thought has taken hold of these souls. It is this which makes it so difficult today to take a position regarding the social question, because such a small possibility exists for the understanding, the mutual understanding of the classes. The middle class has difficulty in placing themselves into the souls of the proletarians, they can hardly understand how it came about, one could call it, that a still unknown mind with an elementary intelligence could find a place such as this — be as it may towards this content — that one can have human thought develop the highest measure for an applied system, like the philosophy of *Karl Marx*.

Certainly, the philosophy of Karl Marx can be accepted by one and rejected by another, perhaps on the same grounds as the other. It may well be revised later for those observing social life after the death of Marx and his friend Engels. I do not wish to speak about the content of this philosophy at all. The most important for me is the fact presented: there worked a forceful thought impulse within the workforce, within the proletarian world. Added to this, one can express it in the following way: a practical movement, a pure philosophy of life with universal human claims has never stood nearly as totally alone based on a purely scientific thought as this modern proletarian movement. It is to some extent the first of its kind of movement in the world based purely on a scientific basis. Nevertheless, if all of this is considered — I've already indicated it — what the modern proletarian expresses about his personal thoughts, desires and experiences seem hardly important when considered through a penetrating examination of life.

Many people have fiercely shown how this modern proletarian social movement originated from the evolution of humanity during the last few centuries. Vehemently it was shown how the development of modern technology in particular, through the development of the modern nature of machines, actually created the proletariat in the modern sense; how through even the forceful scientific turnaround of the new time, it created the social question. Other sharp criticisms about the origin of the social question I do not wish to repeat. However, it seems important to me to characterize the present contradictions in this modern proletarian movement. Certainly, it is important that without the enormous turnaround, without the technical revolution of the new age the modern social movement could not have come to expression to such an extent. However intensively as its origins are claimed out of purely scientific impulses, out of economic powers, out of class clashes and out of class struggles, what is obvious in social life today does not stand as coming from mere scientific oppositions, mere scientific forces if considered through penetrating soul observations of the modern proletariat. Those who are familiar with a spiritual scientific approach who considers all that is human, the refinements and intimacies of soul life, even though these carriers of the soul life are often not conscious, for them it is clear that nothing which is technically or scientifically created has an importance in today's social question but that the facts are important which relate to the entirely different interrelationships in life where some people are involved with machines in the realm of big capitalist enterprises. Through this placement something is awakened in these people that are not directly related to what surrounds them and the economic situation in which they are involved. What is awakened in them is far more connected to the deepest lifetime habits of modern humanity.

If history is only considered in this way, as it wants to do now again in the newer time out of social science which says results follow from what went before — processes always refer to earlier causes — it indicates that forces of change and evolution are not considered as being alive in reality, but are being seen as mere cause and effect — one could call it the sober, arid connection of cause and effect expressed at certain points of its revolutionary development.

Take a single example in human development. For my sake let's take, if we may call it 'successive' development, what happens between birth and the first change of teeth. An enormous transformation takes place in the human body. Just observe what develops during this period of life. There is no obvious straight line connecting cause and effect. Then again, we can consider what happens between the seventh and fourteenth years, fifteen years and so on, in order to follow a straight line of development from cause to effect. Now again a revolutionary formation in the human body takes place towards adolescence. These changes are less obvious later but they are there. Just like such things happen which ruin the repetition of comfortable but inaccurate claims that Nature makes no jumps, jumps that take place in single organisms, it does appear in the historical evolution of humanity. In the time between the middle of the 14th and 15th centuries up to today you have quite powerful evolutionary processes taking place in human consciousness itself.

Just as a single human organism becomes something different after puberty than in the specific direction it had been going before, just so the human social organism has become something different after the elementary, underlying aspects have been validated by not merely following the straight line of cause and effect. Whoever wishes to observe history knows that before present time, humanity reacted instinctively but that now we enter our present time in full consciousness, it must be approached with full awareness. Due to this the social movement takes on a particular characteristic, expressed in a word which does not characterise it intensively enough: proletarian class consciousness. With this expression 'proletarian class consciousness' one should take less into account that it points to a necessary battle where proletarians get mixed up with other classes but rather much more that the social instincts which lived in the souls of the proletarians earlier, have now been transformed into a social awareness. Earlier, class instinct existed. Now the basis of the social movement is class consciousness.

This class consciousness, one could say, is only superficially indicated when one takes the wording: proletarian class consciousness. What is hidden in this expression 'proletarian class consciousness' is something quite different. It could be said — when one wants to briefly characterise this serious fact — within the relationships of historical occupations, for example expressed in the handwork or other crafts of olden days, lies specific social instincts which shone through human souls and worked out of human souls. These instincts enabled a process to be brought about between the way people thought, felt and acted, what they treasured for their honour, their joy and their aesthetic needs. This work itself gave something to the people.

When people were introduced to machines, when they entered into the totally impersonal mechanism of modern capitalism, it was no longer clearly transparent how the remuneration for the human performance was evaluated but monetary increase of capital became most important, so people were driven on the one side by the power of machines and on the other side into modern capitalistic economic regulations, having been torn out of their present day relationship to the world and life which gave them something personal, something towards personal joy, personal honour and personal will impulses. They were to some extent placed on the pinnacle of the personal beside the machine, within the purely objective, impersonal circulation of goods and capital, which they did not basically care for on a human personal level. However, the human soul always strives for fulfilment, wants to unfold its entire circumference. The workers, torn from their characterised other relationships in life, were torn loose from a full human life and were urged to reflect about human dignity, urged to recreate human dignity.

So, hidden behind what we called proletarian class consciousness in modern history's evolution was actually a dawning, a brightening up of a self-created human consciousness out of the souls of the people. Steering the consciousness gave rise to the question: What am I as a human being? What meaning do I have as a human being in the world? — Experiencing this gave the opportunity to proletarians while being positioned beside machines denying humanity, next to capital denying humanity.

I do still believe that the entire consideration of the social question is placed on another basis if one thinks that, while the rest of humanity more or less out of the context of their lives were not brought out of old instincts as radically and revolutionarily and drawn into the modern consciousness, the modern proletarian radically entered into a conscious understanding of themselves, whereas before they had been driven by instincts and human dignity for individuals in the community.

The arrival of consciousness in the soul of proletarians is connected to all kinds of other things which appeared earlier in human evolution. Its arrival coincides with certain steps in human thought, with certain steps in human development. Basically, the historical development of humanity is poorly understood. The historical development of humanity is basically always approached from one or other party. Whoever considers humanity's development objectively often sees it as completely different from how statements are made about this development. One can also say that whoever looks at what presently enjoys the most authority today, namely science, knows, anything proven with absolute objectivity has developed out of a previous element and clearly carries indications of its origin which can in turn take on other forms. If you look at science and its brilliant methods, at its endless conscientious research, so suitable at penetrating the phenomena of nature, then you see that the most pervasive statement it has to admit to is that basically it is hardly appropriate for understanding the deepest, most intimate human feelings and experiences, that it has little to say about actual concerns of the human being when he or she turns their gaze to self-knowledge and mindfulness. Science itself has also to some extent torn itself away from human beings. It no longer carries a personal character and it no longer speaks about the spiritual, super-sensory or eternal in human beings. If science does mention it then it is clearly shown as is the fashion today, that it neither has the corresponding methods nor the corresponding ways to research it.

One can look back to a time when the form of science within the development of humanity was fully integrated in the religious conception of life, with religious experience and scientific observation. The two separated. What was once united split around the same time when this revolution towards objectivity started, the time of machines, when modern capitalism found expression. At the time of this radical scientific change it was also the time religious evolution came to a standstill and did not want to cooperate with scientific developments. At the time Giordano Bruno became criticized over Galileo Galilei (heliocentrism), remnants remained of a withdrawal from intimate human experiences and feelings which needed expression about nature and the world as such. Humanity lost the belief that knowledge could be penetrated with a religious glow, with religious warmth. Today one is proud that science can remain free from all that is blameworthy in religion. During this time when science freed itself more and more from religion, wanting to become free of the spirit, into this time came the development of the proletarian consciousness, the apprehension of the human consciousness through the Proletariat.

Proletarianism penetrated into modern thinking, into modern intelligence, which can be grasped by human intelligence. It founded a science which no longer had the impact to capture and fulfil the whole human being. This resulted in the modern Proletariat having a specific form. The spiritual awareness of humanity, the spiritual consciousness of earlier classes which existed in earlier times lost the impact and human circumstances more or less were delivered to abstract science. Thus, the Proletarians in this new time saw science in opposition to their souls, science which did not instil trust that something can come out of it as a most true, inner spiritual reality living in the outer sensory, scientific activity. This was the type of science the Proletarian confronted, was set against. It lived into human beings. From the spiritual evolutionary basis, something rose up and today appears as a naturalness, as an absolute truth, which can only be recognised in its true nature if you have the ability to see what is happening in the soul of a person. An observer with deeper insight is moved the most by the manner and way which the modern Proletarian talk about actual spiritual affairs, about customs, morality, art, religion, even about science within evolution, that all of this is included by expressions of ideals. This is the most moving. In particular, it is most moving to know that the modern Proletarian clearly believes that everything, from thought, artistic creativity and religious experience actually arises out of the human soul as a falsely created image, an ideology. The actual reality is however scientific battles, economic causes; they represent reality. The reflection within the soul is human evolution, considered as ideological. At least this throws an impulse back into the pure materialistic reality of economic events. Even though it works back on economic events, it still has had its origins developed out of economic events.

This statement about spiritual life living in the modern proletarian question was something far more real than what is thought. Why have art, customs, morality, religion and the spiritual life of the modern Proletarian become an ideology? Because earlier ruling circles presented a science which no longer wanted to uphold a living relationship with the actual spiritual world, a science which no longer pointed to an impulse directed at actual spirituality. Such a science can at most lead to abstract concepts of natural laws. It can lead to nothing other than seeing the spiritual as an ideology. It produces methods which are only suitable on the one side for the purely objective, non-human nature and within human life only as economic events. When the modern proletarian had to take over this direction of science, his gaze was as if conquered by a mighty suggestive power which can only be linked to such a science; the economic life. He now started to believe that this economic life could be the only reality because for him from a civil class, science becomes the directive as the only truth for his economic life.

This was an unbelievably critical element because this gave the proletarian movement its actual characteristic impulse. One can see how old instincts within this proletarian movement were still present, even in the last decades of the 19th Century. One still finds in some proletarian programs such items of discussion on the awareness of man's worth, thc prcoccupation of rights leading to such real worthiness. Since the nineties we see under the influence of this impulse which I've just mentioned, how the Proletarians and their learned advocate glances appear as a powerful persuasive force linked to economic life. They no longer believed a spiritual or soul element from elsewhere needed to enter as an impetus into the realm of the social movement. They believed that only through the development of the un-spiritual, economic life void of soul could a sense of man's worth be brought about. They aimed at revolutionizing economic life to such a degree that all the harm resulting from egoism of single workers in private enterprise would be taken from them and single employers doing justice to the demands of human worth from the side of the employees made impossible. Thus, the Proletarians considered the only salvation to be the transfer of all private property towards a means of production in a communal business or else a common ownership. In addition, this depended basically upon people deviating their gaze from any spiritual or soul elements, regarding the spiritual as mere ideology when there was a purely scientific method, firmly established, which could be steered towards a pure economic process.

A very peculiar fact now transpired, showing how many contradictions lay in this modern proletarian movement. The modern Proletarian believed that the economy itself had to develop in such a way as to finally become a full human right. To acquire human rights as it appeared to him, was what he fought for. However, within his aspiration something appeared which could never have originated if it came only out of economic life. This is an important, penetrating fact of discourse at the centre of various forms of the social question arising from life's necessities of present day humanity which was believed to have come out of economic life itself, but which did not originate from economic life but developed much more during the gradual evolution of the old serfdom of bodily possession during the feudal times leading up to the modern proletarian worker. Just as the circulation of goods, circulation of money, the nature of capital, possession, the nature of land and grounds and so on has developed something out of modern life which cannot be expressed clearly by the modern Proletarian, it is nevertheless clearly experienced as the actual foundation of social will. It is like this: the modern capitalistic economic order basically only knows about its goods within its areas of circulation. It knows about building wealth of goods within the economic organism. It is within the capitalistic organism of the newer age where it has become goods, but the Proletariat feels it may not be goods. However, if he focuses scientifically on economic life he can't say anything but: "It is goods." That is in other words his own labour.

When a person realizes where the basic impulse of the social movement comes from, with his subconscious experiences through his instincts as a modern Proletariat, a disgust grows towards this idea that labour is sold to the employee just like goods, this disgust grows because his labour is dependent on supply and demand, it comes down to disgust for the labour commodity as the actual basic impulse of the modern social movement, when this is impartially considered and not penetrated and radically spoken about adequately as socialistic theories then the point is reached which gives rise to the urgent, nay burning question regarding the social movement.

In olden times, there were slaves. An entire person was sold as goods. In serfdom, a little less of a person was sold, but still nearly the whole person. Capital became the power which made people a form of goods, namely labour. A method needs to be found for dividing the rest of the circulation of goods with labour as goods. Humanity will only realize what hides behind this fact when the economy is not considered through persuasion but through quite another method, when applied to the human being itself, is understood, not out of economy but quite something different flowing in a way which distances the human worker away from the nature of goods. People must realise — and here spiritual scientific research is available as a basis — that the belief is wrong that through the consideration of only the economic system which only fits the scientific method, the way can be found of how the labour of individuals can become members of the social organism. Only when the understanding is reached that labour belongs to the economic system as much as processes in the lung-, heart- and circulatory systems are the same as in the nerves and head system, then one is on the same track. The nervous system and senses centralised in the head is an independent member of the human organism. The lung and heart system are also independent members. Similarly, with the digestive system. These things can be studied more precisely in my book "**Riddles of the Soul**" (Von Seelenrätseln). It is characteristic of the human organism that through their correct development and processes they are not centralised but exist beside one another and work freely together. If one can't understand the human organism in this all-inclusive, penetrating way, then one could through science, which has not been renewed and needs spiritual science to reform it, not understand the social organism correctly. Today it is believed that the human organism is centralised, while it is in fact threefold.

In the same way, the social organism is threefold. Today the powerful persuasion considered as the economic system, is only one member. Another member which needs to come out of this is an understanding of the function of human labour in the entire structure of the social organism. The two systems need to exist side by side. The attribute linked to goods by the labour force is wrongly given by modern thinking. This narrow minded, modern thinking which needs to place the third independent member into the social organism, the spiritual life, is made into a mere ideology. The theoretical view that spirituality is mere ideology, is the most harmless. The important element is that people who have the point of view that the spirit is not rooted at the base of all things in reality, but that it's only an ideology, can't be the real spiritual impulse. Such a person has no interest in his spiritual life allocating his true role in the world. By examining the more modern necessities of life in the proletarian consciousness then one finds no possible insight in the three aspects of the social organism. It was lost to them. Nationalization was striven for because it was believed to be the only social organization which could conquer everything. Spiritual scientific awareness may reveal a wider horizon as even today in this burning time of appointed leaders it is often given with reference to the social question. It needs to be pointed out that what is, is really needed is the necessity to renew thinking, the necessity to not only develop a scientific way of observing social life which is being substituted by traditional science but that it is necessary to recreate a science, a new way of thinking which will become a reality in the social organism, in human consciousness. This will have to lead to so much unhappiness in modern times being removed from consciousness. Those who do not work theoretically but out of life itself, as I believe they have done so during this hour, are also dispatched and made harmless by those who call themselves practical, by saying: ‘Oh, from such theoretical things nothing advantageous comes into the world.’ These people who practice practicality for life, who are the real members of abstractions, these people whose practice is nothing other than the limitation of their senses by the narrowest boundaries, these have caused a multitude of bad luck and catastrophes lately. If they are able to economise further in all party directions, misfortunes will not come to an end but will spread out immensely. The real life-practitioners must maintain their proper positions in the public sphere and speak about developmental possibilities in the spatial and temporal social organism as in the case of every single human being. These real life-practitioners who speak out of a deeper reality are the ones upon whom we may depend. They are the ones who do not need to disbelieve their own knowledge. However, as practical people, also socialistic life practitioners, they see their suffering and their regret on the other side with only the belief that it will lead nowhere else other than to the depletion of life. Those who as life practitioners want to work out of the spirit, strive out of reality towards viable reality.

Regarding the sense in which solutions can be found to the question I attempted out of newer habits of today and revealing their true form, how attempts at finding solutions could be proven on the basis of an examination of the reality of social life and the community's structure of humanity, I will allow myself to speak about, the day after tomorrow.

A COMPARISON BETWEEN THE ATTEMPTS AT SOLVING THE SOCIAL QUESTION BASED ON LIFE'S REALITIES AND THE NECESSITY FOR A SCIENTIFIC SPIRITUAL CONCEPT OF LIFE AS A SOCIAL ORGANISM.

Lecture 2

by Rudolf Steiner

given at Zurich, 5 February 1919

wn.rsarchive.org/Lectures/GA328/English/eLib2017/19190205p01.html

With reference to my presentations I would like to ask you to take these four lectures as a unit. This means the content of one lecture is not to be taken as independent and judged this way. The relative theme is so comprehensive that it can only be manageable by doing a number of lectures.

In today's lecture I would like to make a provisional outline for possible solving techniques distilled from actual knowledge of the being of the social organism, of such solution possibilities for the social question which do not come out of some one-sided remark about some or other class, some or other state, but coming from appropriate reality, coming from the properly observed evolutionary forces of humanity and in particular those evolutionary forces which are the most pronounced at present and valid for the near future of humanity.

If one tries to find a solution for the social question through the aspirations or the demands of a state, of a class, out of some part of the social organism, then one does nothing other than undermine the other elements of the social organism by calling on yet another class which in some way or other restrict development or healthy living conditions.

For our time here, it is relevant to reveal and substantiate my indications of truths in the following lectures. In modern life, or it could be called the modern social organism, quite a particular form is experienced through expressions characteristic of modern life, through technology, through the technical operation of economic life and its relationships and through the capitalistic process which organises this economic enterprise. Not necessarily only those with a conscious focus observe this modern technology and modern capitalism as they were introduced into life, but their focus was on the more or less conscious or the more or less instinctive, actively organised forces within the social structure of the human community.

The characteristic, particular form of the social question coming to the fore in modern times can be expressed as follows: economic life supported by technology and modern capitalism have worked in a natural self-evident way and brought order into the modern community. Besides this claim for human awareness towards technology and capitalism, the awareness was deflected by other branches, other spheres of the social organism, where awareness should have become as necessary as the health of the social organism as it was with the economic field.

Perhaps I may use a comparison to clearly communicate what I could call the nerve of a comprehensive, many-sided observation of the social question. Please consider that with a comparison I don't mean anything other than a support of human understanding in order to orientate it towards the healing of the social question. Whoever wants to consider what we know as the most complicated organism — that of the human being — needs to pay attention to the existence of three operative systems working side by side in the human form. These three cooperative systems can be characterised in the following way. One could say in the human, natural organism a system works incorporating the nerves and senses. One could call the most important member of this system where the nerves and senses are centralized, the head organisation.

As to the second member of the human organism, in order to develop a real understanding of this organism it is necessary to consider what I would like to call the rhythmic system, in relationship with breathing, blood circulation and everything expressed as rhythmic processes. As a third system, one can recognise all the organs whose actions relate to metabolism. In these three systems are the combined effects, when they interact in a healthy way, of all that is contained in the human organism. I have tried, in full agreement with all the research science has claimed, to characterise this threefold aspect of the human being as an outline in my book "**Riddles of the Soul**" I am clear about all the aspects to be introduced in the future by biology, physiology and science regarding the human organism which will see how this threefold head-, circulation-, (or chest system) and digestive systems are maintained — that these members each work in a particular independent way which indicates it is not an complete centralisation of the organism. These three systems each have a particular relationship to the outer world; the head system through the senses, the circulation or rhythmic system through breathing and the digestive system through the nutritional organs. In relation to scientific methods we have not progressed as far as these ideas I'm indicating here, out of spiritual scientific foundations for natural science as I've tried to use, in order to present it in scientific circles as a general statement and in a way, make it desirable for the evolution of knowledge. This means however that our thinking habits, the entire way we imagine the world to be has not completely been adjusted to the example of the human organism as it is presented in its natural processes. In a way one could say yes, science can wait, they may gradually rush to their ideals, they will soon come to the view that such observations are their own. However, regarding the examination and especially the processes of the social organism, one can't wait. Not with some or other expert but for every human soul — because every human soul shares in the work of the social organism — at least must take part in the work of the social organism — at least by an instinctive knowledge of the necessities of this social organism. Healthy thought and experience, a healthy will and desire in relation to the expression of the social order can only develop when people — whether more or less instinctive — can understand that this social organism, if it is to be healthy, must be a natural threefold organism.

Now I am at the point where I need to be very careful not to be misunderstood. Since *Schäffle* wrote a book about the social organism, there have been repeated attempts at establishing an analogy between a natural organization, let's say an organisation of people, and on the other side, a human community as such. So many efforts have been made to determine the cell of the social organism, where the cell structure exists, what the tissues could be and so on! Recently a book appeared by Aleray, "Weltmutation" (mutation of the world), in which certain scientific facts and scientific laws are simply transferred on to, what they call, the social organization. With all these analogy games, nothing relates to what we are considering here. Those who at the end of this lecture could say: 'Oh, here we have yet again such a game of analogy between the natural organism and the social organism' — would prove that the real spirit within the meaning has not been penetrated by the listener. This I don't want — some or other scientific facts adjusted as truth and transplanted on to the social organisation. What I want is for human thinking, human feeling to learn through observation of the natural organism that this method, this way of sensing can in turn be applied to the social organization. When you simply take the belief you learnt about natural organisms and apply that to social organism, like Schäffle has done, like others have done too, likewise with "Weltmutation" then it shows you are unwilling to develop a capability to consider the social organism as independent, to examine it as such, to research it according to its own laws, just as you do with natural organisms. In order for you to understand me I have made this comparison with a natural organism. The very moment you continue, like the researcher in nature, objectively meeting the natural organism, as you would place yourself before the independence of the social organism in order to learn about its laws, in that moment the game of analogy regarding the earnestness of your observation, will stop.

I want to call your attention now to how this play of analogies must come to an end. The examination of the social organism — here it involves something becoming, something which must come into existence first — in as far as it must be healthy, leads to the three members of this social organism, but they both can only be recognised as independent as such, when considered objectively. On the one side, you can distinguish three members of the human organism, on the other side the objective, independent members of the social organism. If you look for analogies, then you most likely will experience the following. You would say that this human head- or nerve-system relates to human spiritual life with its spiritual abilities; the circulatory system rules the relation with this spiritual system with the crudest system, and the materialistic system with the digestive system. The digestive system could be considered through certain fundamental experiences as the crudest of systems in the human organism. What then, if you continued the game of analogy, would be the next thing?

The next thing would be to say the social organism divides into three branches.

Spiritual life develops within a person. That is one member. Within a person his actual political life develops too — we will speak about this division of branches afterwards — and also his economic or business life develops within. You could, if you wanted to play the analogy game, believe that spiritual life as in spiritual culture in the social organism is subject to the same kind of laws which allow a comparison with the laws in the nervous and sense systems. The system considered as unrefined, the most materialistic, the digestive system, can in the game of analogy probably be compared with what one calls the crude system of material business life. Whoever can consider things for themselves and stay far away from the mere game of analogy will know that in reality, things are actually reversed in comparison with what comes out of mere analogy. See, the social organism lies opposite the economic production and consumption, opposite the economic circulation of goods at the basis of life's rules, just like the natural human organism's laws are at the foundation of the nerves- and sense-life, which is its spiritual system. Certainly the life of public law, the actual political life, life which is often too all-encompassing, which can be described as the actual civil life, allows itself to be between the two systems of the digestive and the nerve-sense systems where the rhythmic system lies, the regulating system of the breathing and heart. Only by comparing how the human organism has, between its digestive and nerve-systems the central circulation or rhythmic systems, so between the public rights and the economic system stand the actual life of spiritual culture. This life of spiritual culture, this spiritual life of the social organism has no laws which can be thought of as analogous to laws of human talents, laws of human sense and nerve existence but the spiritual life in the social organism has laws which can only be compared with laws in the crudest system, the metabolic system.

This leads to an objective observation of the social organism. Regarding this particular point the assumption must be clear in order for no misunderstanding to arise in a belief that the physiological or biological elements are simply transferred on to the social organism. The social organism must be considered as an independent organism throughout for its success towards recovery to take place. In various areas in central and eastern Europe the word "socializing" is heard. This socializing will not become a healing process but a fake process in the social organism, perhaps even a disturbing process if the human heart, the soul does not have insight with instinctive knowledge of the necessity for a threefoldness in the social organism. This social organism has in every case, if it is to work in a healthy way, three members. The first member, to begin with from the one side — one could understandably also start on the side of the spiritual life but for now we will start on the economic side as this obviously controls the rest of life through modern technology in modern capitalism — therefore, the first member of the social organism as business life, or economic life, will be looked at. This economic life, we will partly today and partly in the course of these lectures see it has to be an independent member within the social organism just as in comparison, the nerve- sense system is relatively independent in the human organism. Our economic life is connected to all that takes place in the production, circulation and consumption of goods. With everything connected to these three things, economy is linked. We will soon consider its characteristics in order to understand it more closely.

As a second member of the social organism we observe the life of public law, the actual political life, for the purposes of the old constitutional state it could be called the actual life of the state. Meanwhile economic life involves the business of everything which the human being brings out of nature as his own production, because the economic life involves the circulation and consumption of goods, so this second member of the social organism is involved with everything with a human foundation with its relationships of people with people. This I ask you to consider comprehensively, because it is important for knowledge of the members of the social organism to know the difference between public laws which relate to the foundation of one human being to another, while in the economic system it involves the production, circulation and consumption of goods. One must be able to distinguish between the natural human system in relation to the lungs and outer air, the processing of this outer air, how this differs from the manner and way nourishment is transformed in the third natural system within the human being.

As a third member which must be placed independently from the others, there has to be a distinction from everything in the social order which involved spiritual life. More precisely the name 'spiritual culture' does not cover everything connected to spiritual life; it should be everything flowing into the social organism which depends on the natural gift of individuals, the natural spiritual and physical talents coming from single individuals. Similar to the first system, the economic system which needs to exist for humanity to relates and regulates the outer world, the second system which must exist in the social organism, relates to everything happening between one person and another; there we have the third system. In order for this third system to have a name it will be called the spiritual system, involved with everything which is created out of the single human individuality and needing to be incorporated into the social organism.

Even as true as it is that modern technology and modern capitalism have given a stamp to our modern community life, it actually is so necessary for the wounds of humanity beaten from this side to be healed and thus enable people and communities to develop the right relationship to the threefold social order I am characterizing here.

Economic life has in our modern time taken on particular forms. It has so to speak penetrated human life with its own rules. Both the other members of the social organism are in the position to bring their own independent laws in the right way into this social organism. For them it is necessary that people out of independence and from a point of awareness carry out the social membership, each in its place, where it is positioned. For the purpose of finding solutions to the social question which we are considering, every single person has a social task in the present and near future. The first member of the social organism, the economic life, rests primarily on a natural background. Just as each individual depends for his learning and his education on the talents of his spiritual and physical organs, on those gifts and talents given to him, likewise economic life depends on certain natural foundations. This natural basis gives economic life — and through this the totality of the social organism — its character. However, these natural foundations are there without having to be discovered through some social organisation, some or other socializing of its original form. This needs consideration. Just as with the education of humanity the various gifts they have need consideration, in natural bodily and spiritual abilities, so every attempt at socializing community living by giving it an economic form as well, need consideration out of its natural foundations. All circulation of goods and also all human labour and any spiritual cultural life lie at the foundation of the first elementary origins chained by human beings to a particular part of nature. Here one needs to really think about the social organism's relationship with the natural foundation, for instance as in individuals in regard to learning and education, in relation to their gifts in thinking. This can be made clear by taking extreme examples.

For instance, you can imagine how in various parts on earth, locally produced bananas present a source of nourishment, how bananas quality in the community to be displaced from their point of origin and be made into a consumable product at a specific destination. Compare the human labour involved in making bananas into consumables for the community with the work of making wheat into a consumable product in the vicinity of Central Europe, it is clear the work needed for the bananas, modestly calculated, is three hundred times less. The work necessary to make the wheat consumable is, lightly calculated, three hundred times bigger.

This is indeed an extreme example. Such differences regarding the measure of work necessary in relation to its natural origin exist in our production line also, under the production line which is represented in some or other social organism in Europe. Not as radical a difference as between bananas and wheat, but the differences are there. Just as the economic organism is founded on the relationship between human beings and their consumption of nature, the measure of the work talents in reality dependent on the natural origin, so the being of a person is dependent on his natural physical or spiritual gifts. One can make a comparison. In Germany, in the region of middle profit abilities, the sowing of wheat has a crop return of seven to eight times at the harvest. In Chile this becomes twelve times, in north Mexico seventeen times and in Peru twenty times, south Mexico twenty-five times up to thirty-five times. For different regions of the earth the return in wheat productivity is in relation to the earth, to the yield of the earth. This actually affects the measure of labour needed to bring the wheat in an appropriate manner into the economic life.

Just as one can make such data for the measure of labour needed to process the wheat into a consumable item in different regions, so comparisons can be made for the labour needed in the most varied production lines, raw materials with different production lines made consumable within the economic sphere of a social organism.

This whole interconnected being found in the preliminary processes at the beginning of the relation of people to nature, which continue in every human action by transforming products of nature into consumables for the community, all these processes which are involved as a whole from the natural foundations up to consumables, all these processes, and only these, are included in a healthy social organism as a pure economic member of the social organization. This economic member of the social organisation must be — I will in the course of the lectures give more details with proof — with just such an independence be positioned in the whole social organism as the human head organisation stands in relation to the entire human organism.

Independently standing beside the economic system another system must exist and that is the relationship between one person and another. Living within the purely economic system is the relationship which needs to be established between people and objective goods. A healthy social life needs to develop as a second member of the social organism which regulates everything in relationships between one person and another.

People have neglected achieving the correct difference between the two members of the social organism through the hypnotic belief that modern technology and ancient thinking habits in modern times are the economic forces and processes necessary, either for single regions or in the radical social sense, which can be transformed into the totality of economic life, applied to what I have here as the second member, as the actual state region in a narrower sense, as the region of public law, as the area of relationships between one person to the other.

This region of the state can only then develop in a healthy way when the conflicting streams of development cut in, which are considered by some as correct. Many people believe that healing the social organism is only achievable through nationalization as much as possible; with the greatest degree of association with nationalism — but it involves far more the necessity for complete autonomy, acknowledged and applied to all the separate branches of life, which must step in between economic life — with all its laws on the one side — and the narrower life of the state on the other side — again with its own laws.

I can well imagine how many people there are who say: 'For Heavens' sake, these things are becoming so complicated! Things which are brought together out of necessities for new developments are now to be separated from one another by various systems!' Whoever speaks in this way, unable to consider origins developing in a natural way, would even refuse to understand that the human organism can only be alive as a result of the relative autonomy of the rhythmic life, the vital breathing and hart in the breast, concentrated, centralized in the breathing and in the heart system. The entire human organism is dependent on such systems being closed in and yet working together. The health of the social organism depends on the economic life having its own laws, that the legal life, the life of public law and public security, everything fitting the narrower description of political, has its own laws and its own proficiencies. Only then will both these spheres work in the right way, in the social organism. May it come about with some, who believe certain requirements have finally been accomplished, while others may well raise a shoulder, that it can eventually be said: no healing in the central management of the social organism, as within a party, can happen without cooperation between economic life and political life. If this does happen we will see it is valid for the third member as well. It is necessary nonetheless, that just as the circulatory system has its own lungs, just as the nerve-sense system has its own brain system, so in a single management system its own management, an autonomous replacement system or party or other representation is there for the economic and political or public legal systems, and then again for the third domain, an autonomous area for spiritual life.

These three spheres have a valid autonomy in a healthy organism and relate to one another through their independent representative, enabling this mutual relationship between the three members of the social organism. This corresponds to them in the same way as the independent relationship is produced by the three members of the natural human organism. It turns out that essentially those representations and administrations produced out of the economic members of the organism, that these essentially work towards the economic organism building an associated foundation for itself, a cooperative, trade unionism, but in a higher form. This cooperative trade unionism will only work with the laws of production, work with the circulation and consumption of goods. This is what creates the foundation, builds the content for the economic member of the social organism. It will depend on the vitality of association. It will depend on those who have given the necessary inequality produced from natural foundations, to balance it out. I have pointed out how many variations exist in the amount of human labour needed according to different relationship of the natural source of a member's production. All this enters into an unnatural social organization, when such cooperation is achieved as it has been up to now, of nature, human labour and capital. In a most chaotic way nature, human labour and capital are infused into a unified state or remain outside lawlessly, outside this unitary state. Even though the life of spiritual culture which is dependent on people's physical and spiritual talents for their expression, so also the chosen public and political laws of life must be acknowledged for their need to develop an independent life for themselves, such as the economic system.

I could, to make myself better understood as far as it is needed today, include the following. Besides other foundations out of which we live today, there is also a surfacing out of mankind's deep, natural foundations for a renewal of the social organism, in which can be heard the three words: brotherhood, equality, freedom. Whoever is unprejudiced towards a healthy human experience for all that is really human, will not feel anything but the deepest sympathy and deepest understanding for the meaning in the words, brotherhood, equality, and freedom. Nevertheless, I know of extraordinary thinkers, deep astute thinkers who repeatedly in the course of the 19th Century took the trouble to show how impossible it is to make a united social organism comprising brotherhood, equality and freedom, a reality. An astute Hungarian searched for proof that these three things, but when they are realized, when they penetrate human social structure, they will contradict themselves. Shrewdly he referred to the example of how impossible it is to instil equality into social life because every human being also wants the necessity for freedom to be valid. He found these three ideals to be contradictory. Interestingly, one can't but agree that there is a contradiction and one can't but sympathise out of a general human experience regarding these three ideals. Why these?

Because as soon as the true sense of these three ideals become clear, it will be recognised as necessarily a threefold social organism. The three members should not be an abstract, theoretical parliament or some unit assembled and centralized, they should be living reality and through their lively activity side by side be brought together in a unit. When these three members are independent they contradict one another in a certain way, just like the metabolic system is at variance with the head and rhythmic systems. However, in life, contradictions are just what work together in a unit. Through an understanding of life, one is able to figure out the real gesture of the social organism. A realization will arise that brotherliness must be active in order for cooperation within economic life, where rules are needed among one another regarding particulars, are to be created in this first social member. In the second member of public law where it deals with the relationship of one person to another, only in as far as a human being is a person, it works with the activation of the idea of equality. In the spiritual sphere, where again it has to exist independently in the social organism, it deals with the idea of freedom. Now suddenly the three golden ideals gain their real value when it is known that they may not reach success through an inter-scrambled mixture but that they are orientated according to laws within the threefold organism in which each single one of the three members can achieve its applicable ideal of freedom, equality and brotherhood.

Today I can only propose the structure of the social organism in the form of a sketch. In the following lectures, I will substantiate and prove each one individually. Adding to what has been said is a third member of a healthy social organism with everything arising out of the human individuality, on the foundation of freedom and based on the physical and spiritual gifts of individuals. Here again an area is touched which causes quiet shudders when things are truthfully defined. To continue with this healthy organism, a third area is added which encompasses everything which relates to the religious life of humanity, everything related to schools and education in the widest sense which includes spiritual life, the practice of art and so on. While I only want to mention this today, in the next lectures I will create an extensive foundation regarding everything which belongs to this third sphere — which is not related to public law which belongs in the second sphere — but which is related to private law and criminal law. I found with those to whom I've explained this threefold social organism and who have understood some of it, that they could not grasp the idea that public law, the law which relates to the security and equality of people, should be separated from the right towards law breaking, or towards the private relationships between people; that this could be regarded as separate, and private law and criminal law must be included in the third, in the spiritual member of the social organism.

Modern life has unfortunately turned away from considering these three members of the social organism. Just like the body of economics with its concerns have penetrated into the government, into actual political life, penetrated its concerns into the representative body of political life, the result has clouded the possibility for the second member of the organism to be formed in which human equality can be realized, so too the economic and public life have absorbed the possibility which can only develop itself in a freer form. Out of a certain instinct, out of an erroneous instinct however, modern social democracy has tried to separate religious life from the life of the public state: "Religion is a private affair"; unfortunately, not out of particular care for religion, not out of a special evaluation accessible through the religious life, but out of disregard, out of complacency towards religious life linked to the content I presented in my previous lecture, the day before yesterday. This progression is right for the separation of religious life from the other spheres, from the formation of the economic life and from the formation of political life. Just as necessary as the separation of the lower and higher educational systems are, so too is the spiritual life actually from the two other members. A really healthy social organism can only develop when within these entities they ensure equality of all people before the law, when only out of these entities it is ensured that free human individualities develop schools, religious and spiritual life, when it is ensured that life is developed in freedom and no claim is made according to economic or state rules placed on school, educational and spiritual life.

That sounds radical today. Such radicalism must be expressed as soon as it is detected. Spiritual life, inclusive of education, inclusive of jurisdiction in public and criminal matters, actually underlies the complete freedom flowing out of single individuals which both the other members of the social organism can have no influence upon in its configuration, upon its forms.

Yesterday I only offered a sketch towards the direction thinking can move in the search for solutions of the social question, attempts at solutions based on necessities of life, not based on abstract demands of a single party, of a single class, but based on the powers actually developing in modern people.

I wish to say I can understand every objection raised but ask you to wait with objections until my sketch has been carried to completion in my coming lectures. Particularly today I can understand objections being raised as I'm just trying to characterise; the evidence of the World Trade Organization is not yet clear. I must say I can understand every objection coming out of various experiences which I want to represent here with ideas which I believe I can recognise in frequently misjudged spiritual science as the actual foundations of life which I have related to these things.

Behind us lie a time containing the most terrible human catastrophe. Within the life we had to lead within this catastrophic time, we have not had the human heart in the right place if our vision did not contain the power and ability to say: 'Where can we find help out of this terrible chaos into which we have been driven?' — I told you the day before yesterday I would speak about the particular relationships of these wars to their causes and their unfolding in relation to the social question in both my following lectures. Today I would like to say it is clear to me, as we are going to be within these events for a long time to come, events now having entered a crisis which some short-sighted thinkers believe are soon at an end, that out of these things, out of chaos, out of the terrible catastrophe in some or other area of the civilized world it is possible to find the correct thoughts, the correct picture of more truthful, more realistic impulses for the human social organism. Towards various personalities who have been active and advisory during the last years within these terrible events, I have proposed what is also the vein of my various presentations here: I have tried to make it clear to these personalities who are involved, how different events would have been if from an authoritative place in the world it was said: 'We want to head towards a healthy social goal.' — The entire interrelationship of states would have been different if, instead of mere laws and state programs being introduced, a comprehensive program for people in the way indicated here, had been introduced.

One can say that these things have been understood in a certain theoretical way. The content of my lectures has appeared to some in a really sympathetic way. The bridge which needs to be established between understanding such content and the will to actually do something to make it a reality in actual life, each in its own place, this bridge is quite another matter. This would mostly have an uncomfortable effect. For this reason, they compose themselves and say: 'It all sounds a bit like a dream to me, quite impractical.' — They remain calm only because they don't have the will forces to really involve themselves with the course of events. Not a revolutionary course of events is *meant* here, not something which should happen from one day to the next, but a direction in which all single measures of public and private life should be brought for healing, to form a healthy social organism. The content of my lecture the day before yesterday, I have brought in another form to some people on whom one wanted to depend during these difficult times, addressed in the following way: Today, I would say for example, we are in the most terrible time of the war. Expressing the social necessity in this, the most terrible time of The War, it would be to say: People who are committed to this or that state into giving humanity a worthy self-realization which will become a reality for humanity, will enable this terrible course of events to take on quite a different, healing direction than merely the sword, the cannons and such like, or offer nothing through existing regional politics. I say they have the choice to either acknowledge what is offered here out of the developmental conditions and developmental forces within humanity, or to stand alone.

Today we stand, because during the last decade humanity has somehow missed acknowledging the essence of these things, today we stand in front of the most terrible catastrophe which has broken out like a plague, an illness attacking an organism which has failed to live according to its natural laws. This war catastrophe should now clearly reveal what is necessary for the healing of the social organism of humanity. This indication could have been perceived before the war but then it was not so clear, not even recognised. To some I have said: You have been given these indications regarding human evolution in the social sphere which will be brought into a reality in the next twenty to thirty years in the civilized world. I'm not talking about a program or ideal but it is the result of observation of those who want to make a reality of the seed towards an inclination already in humanity today, towards the next ten, twenty or thirty years. You have only to choose, I say, either to work through to its realization with reason, or to face revolutions of social cataclysms, terrible social upheavals. No third choice is possible. The war will probably be the time — so I say to some — where reason is acceptable. After that it could be too late. It is not a program which can be implemented or left undone, but involves recognising something which needs implementation through people, because in it lie their necessary historical growth forces for the future.

Another particular obstacle towards understanding is some or other belief that these things only relate to an inner structure of some state or some human territory. No, such social thoughts are at the same time the basis for the real necessary transformation of outer politics of states under one another. Just like the human organism turns each of its particular organs to the outside world, so also can a state only accomplish it when — if I might use this whole expression — such a social organism can shift its three members into outer activity. Relationships between one individual state and another appear quite different when a centralized government and administrations no longer remain in connection with one another but when one socially educated representative with a spiritual life relate to another representative with a spiritual life in another social state; whether it be an economic or a political representative, corresponding to the representative in the other state. When there is an intermixing, a confused mess due to the three members working outwardly in such a way to create an ensuing conflict at its boundary through the chaos of this intermixing of the three members, then, when across the boundary an independent state with threefold representatives working independently, the process of one member in the international relationship will not only be disrupted by the other, but by contrast, will balance out and be corrected.

This is what I wanted to sketch for you today to support the idea that it doesn't merely involve an assertion of inner social structure of one state but involves the international and social life of humanity. I have already tried to make all these things clear while we are in the middle of these horrific catastrophic events. At the moment, terrible misfortune has broken out over many people in central and eastern Europe, terrible misfortune for every individual, for every perceptive person the rest of the world indicates threatening misfortune. This must take place in relation to the real understanding of humanity for their tasks in the present and future: whoever wants to bring about a healing of life out of the actual evolutionary elements in humanity must take this up, not as an impractical ideal but as an actual practical application in life.

The obvious form modern life has taken on through technology and capitalism has to stand in opposition to the most inner human initiative forms of the spiritual, independent spiritual culture and independent state culture, which bring about in actual fact an equality between one person to another and which also, as we will soon see, could regulate labour and wage relations in a desirable way for the Proletariat.

The question about the form or human labour, about the liberation of labour from goods will only become detachable when threefoldness enters the social organism. The desire of the modern socialist is certainly legitimate as a desire; what they consider a remedy would work the least effectively as a remedy when it transforms outer reality in the way they want it to be.

This I need to stress yet again: I am not trying to come from some one-sided class or party position but from the side of the observation of human developmental forces in order to speak about what some call social integration and others call the healing of social life and others the reawakening of a healthy political sense, and so on.

What we are dealing with here is not some random program but the deepest true impulses coming to the fore in the next decades in humanity's evolution, it is actually the very foundation of the entire meaning and intention which I want to make into a reality with these lectures; it doesn't relate to the opinion of a person from this standpoint, but it relates to the expression of the deepest wishes in mankind for the next decades. This I would like to found and implement and prove in my lectures during the week ahead.

FANATICISM VERSUS A REAL CONCEPTION OF LIFE IN SOCIAL THINKING AND WILLING.

Lecture 3

by Rudolf Steiner

given at Zurich, 10 February 1919

wn.rsarchive.org/Lectures/GA328/English/eLib2017/19190210p01.html

During the lectures last week, I pointed out that the present social situation, particularly where restrictions and difficulties have been experienced during its development, have made an understanding between different classes of humanity today something which lie relatively far into the future. The ruling class, as it has developed during the last century, the last decades up to the present, has its particular thought habits, particular inner impulses forming a basis for its thinking and willing. One could say an abyss exists between thought habits and what I characterized last week, this having developed out of quite a specific peculiarity in thought habits of the modern Proletarians, in whom the actual origin lies in what we call the social question today.

Whoever makes the effort to penetrate the reality of life, the forces playing into communal human relationships, for them it appears far more important what happens within the awareness of people, one could call it, among those who want to consciously discuss the underlying impulses rather than see how they actually arise in consciousness. One can get various views according to middle class thinking circles. Reports on the views of proletarian personalities or proletarian rulers are available; not much of their actual view on life and their creation of criticism about social facts of the present day are to be found here, but more what lies to a certain extent behind these observations. Behind that lies far more social psychology and social soul wisdom than you actually realize, on both sides.

Whoever — I may say it about myself, by presenting these things here — whoever takes the trouble to penetrate from all sides into the thought habits of the bourgeois circle leaders on the one side and on the other the soul impulses of the up-and-coming Proletarians, know how big the cleft is between them, how difficult understanding is; this failure to understand is both a world historic and also a social fact of the present day. We can see this in Paris, in Bern. When one has an ear for such things, one could say that in both places various languages are spoken. At both places, such different languages are spoken that one could doubt that the one spoken at the one place also seems to be most remotely felt by the other, and vice versa. For this reason, it is also so difficult in the present to connect the bourgeois circles to those of the Proletarians and to those things which are the actual main driving forces related to the social question. All that has happened before in history is not quite important but among the historic events are those which point significantly to the actual effective, truly effective powers. Other phenomena which the superficial observer might value as equally important, can in true reality hardly be considered.

Whoever properly pursues the proletarian movement as it has developed over the last decades, a significant fact, one among many, will stand out, that the modern Proletarian, considered in a really, one could call it, in a scientific form which it has taken on, that the actual impulse of this modern proletariat, through their observations, know what to say about things introduced into the present where their solutions must be found just like economic- and community building in the old populace classes had been created and gradually had to disappear to make place for something new to come into existence.

A fact is presented here which has attracted some sceptics. Considering the sceptics will not be considered here, instead we will refer to the historical importance of this matter.

By exploring insightful representatives of the modern proletarian world view, perhaps particularly during the first years when this movement became known when it was examined more at that time than later, one felt more involved in these things, one felt more resigned, but the question still arose: 'What form of community, of human community-living and human actions, what form of the social organism can actually be observed within this view of life as something which must emerge, as something which should be brought about?' — From their point of view the proper answer would be: 'At the moment this is of no further interest to us. Of importance to us above all is to bring a solution to the modern social order which enables it to steer itself ad absurdum. What will happen then, will reveal itself soon enough.' — People are always preoccupied with representing their opinion; the modern proletariat must impress positions of power and control. The overpowering of the marching classes favours him so that when he has power in hand he doesn't need to think, provisionally.

That was programmatic. This is not actually properly thought through. It also invites agitation and is not thought through as a reality. Actually, for those who have a sense for evolutionary powers in history this is the question: 'Yes, what does this modern proletarian point of view actually mean within the evolution of humanity at the present time?' — The result is we are repeatedly distracted, as we said; the point of view takes on less importance as we are distracted about what people have to say about their feelings, how they experience their own lives, how they think about other classes in humanity. Briefly, we are distracted from the proletarian question about the status of the proletarians' lives. To a certain extent not talk nor statements but the particular kind of existence of a class of people show what is important through the way it is expressed. The answer which represents actual reality, given by the actual living proletariat today, can be formulated in the following way. It can be said: 'This modern proletariat with their opportunities in life, with their living conditions, with the manner in which they are positioned in the modern social order and how they feel within themselves, this modern proletarian experience themselves as the criticism of modern technology, capitalism and the economic order.' This is, in my view, extraordinarily interesting, that if you have a sense for reality based observation, that the proletariat themselves have the answer and that it does not come from some or other theoretical analysis, but out of the Proletarians themselves. It is a criticism. That the modern proletarians have become this way is provided by the criticism in a way outside of the proletariat who now take it as payment developed in the modern economic order.

Because this is so the souls of these modern proletarians were particularly open to embark on an abstract teaching, one can call it a teaching on scientific stilts, a teaching permeated by an impulse as I've characterised it, which is actually an impulse out of the life of the modern proletariat: the teaching of Marxism, the teaching of *Karl Marx*. It is a unique example in the history of humanity that such an unused class, a class without decadence, with unused intellectuality, with so much heart and such an open soul, that such a class where there were active forces in their own life forces, that it could have accepted such a scientific theory as happened with the modern proletarians and the Marxist teaching.

One needs to study things in life in this kind of relation. One must have seen how even the most difficult, seen from other classes as respectfully difficult, this has entered into the elementary sensitive and sentient proletarian soul, how millions upon millions of the modern proletarians were gripped by an apparent theoretic teaching.

However, what lives in this theoretic teaching? Here is a strange thing — it does not live in what one could in the ordinary sense call a social ideal. What lives in it doesn't have any formulation that would resemble a future state or a future social structure, but in it exist a real criticism of the modern bourgeois social and economic order and it relates to some extent to the instinct of these Marxist teachings. This instinct can be considered as follows: If I point out to the proletarian what the criticism of the modern technical capitalistic economic order is, then I involve his very life forces, then I steer it towards this becoming his own reality. It is already in a certain sense a mirror image expressed by the direct proletarian life entering right into the Marxist teaching. Whoever believes that the Marxist teaching is dismissed by the proletarian, does not understand that the formulation, the specific point of view and thoughts on the one side, can be overcome. What remains, however, is a certain momentum of this specific impulse which is alive and that on the other side perhaps in a counter observation, is realised by those who have come out of Marxism; that in all kinds of revisionist attempts there is an evolution of the impulse in the modern proletarian introduced through Marxism. This characterization of the social facts in the present time is more important for me than going along with elementary discussions because they eventually lead towards social psychology. When a direct answer is not found — we will encounter this in the course of the lectures what possible answer could be given — then it points to the present question of viewpoints which in real life at present probably will be the first consideration. What kind of experience is had when these things are considered without bias, without prejudice? The result is an experience of a certain peculiarity of modern life. Modern life —

as I have often stressed in the lectures I'm giving here in Zurich — has thought habits, has developed thought forms which prove extremely fruitful for a certain direction in science. These modern thoughts also want to penetrate the understanding and comprehensive reformation, reforming the understanding of the social life itself, the social phenomena and impulses of life. However, with this penetration one has the general feeling that humanity at present, standing within the thought forms and thought habits of today, are not able to grasp the reality of complicated phenomena in social life. To some extent their understanding is too closely meshed. They can't grasp the complicated phenomena of the social life by themselves. They remain abstract, they remain delineated and they don't allow events in the social sphere to enter into actual life itself. One could say tightly meshed thinking characterises modern humanity. This narrow thinking breaks in everywhere where one wants to enter into real life, this very thinking has infiltrated into the ambition of the modern proletarian. The result is that this kind of thinking becomes transformed into criticism and does not enable real impulses created out of human soul experiences to be established as directional forces able to lead into the future. Everywhere this thinking breaks in where there is a striving for such impulses.

This calls for something which is deeply decisive in life at present. Whoever is, in full earnestness, able to understand the need of life at present, may direct his focus from the point of view being considered here, just now within this world historic moments where there is little time for a mere theoretical trend in true discussions because the facts are urgent and burning. Just right now one sees how people are presented with these urgent and burning facts but how even in these thought images it shows that reality can't be penetrated. Many people are filled with good will but not in one of them has thinking processes grown out of these facts. It is obvious in these world historic moments that even for those who wish to penetrate earnestly into this moment in time, the rising up — often masked in a variety of forms, completely unconsciously — of this incline in people for who the true earnest direction in life, when burning and urgent questions appear, it becomes particularly disastrous: the rising up of a type of fanaticism, as I would like to call it. This fanaticism shows itself in the most varied masks in a variety of areas and this makes it so difficult to allow the present to be directed into the appropriate action. This fanaticism has been the result of the development I have indicated historically in my lectures of the previous week, which started at the turning point of the 14th, 15th and 16th Centuries. What is the essence of this fanaticism? The essence can be depicted through a certain unrealistic view of life, a view of life which omits what I called last week the thrust received from inner experiences, through a certain view of life of a soulful, thoughtful and scientific knowledge seeking inner life like searching for an island — or actually an abundance of islands — and failing to build bridges to actualities in everyday life. We find in the present time certainly many people — if I could use the expression — who inwardly find a distinguished manner of thinking, be it in a scholarly abstract way, of all kinds of ethic-religious problems in cloud cuckoo land. One can observe how people ponder about the manner and way in which people could acquire virtues, how they should relate through love with their fellow human beings, how they can become blessed. We notice how concepts of salvation, mercy and so on develop in which certain adherents of this view of life possibly only want to be in the soul spiritual heights. Simultaneously we see in those good people mentioned legally and morally, who are loving and full of goodwill the inability to establish the real bridge to outer reality, everyday circulation of capital, the cost of labour, consumption, production in relation to the circulation of goods, credit systems, banking and stock exchange systems. We see how two streams have developed side by side in the world, reflected also in thought habits: one world movement wants to remain in soul spiritual heights and does not want to build bridges between what is seen as a religious order and the management of ordinary trade. Life however is uniform. It can only unfold when the driving forces of all ethical religious aspects work from its basis into the everyday, profane situation of life, into life which appears even less distinguished. If we neglect to create these bridges we lapse, in relation to the religious and moral life, into mere fanaticism, remote from daily reality, then true everyday reality retaliates. Then people strive out of a certain religious impulse towards all possible ideals, everything which can be called "good," but instincts which oppose daily satisfaction coming from everyday experiences of life which should arise from the national economy, these instincts are powerless in the face of insensitive people. No bridge can seemingly be built between the belief of godly grace and everyday life as it happens. Everyday life then takes revenge. Now everyday life takes on a form which has nothing to do with ethical impulses cherished in distinguished, soul spiritual heights. Revenge becomes such that the ethical religious life, while it distances itself from the everyday things, from direct practical life, that this ethical religious life actually turns surreptitiously — without one noticing it as it is masked — into an inner delusion.

We see how people go about out of a certain ethical religious dignity — they believe — and how they show only the best of will in relation to the community of fellow human beings, a display of the best will to do their utter best towards them, while they neglect actually doing anything, because they have acquired nothing socially in their life of feeling which relate to practical habits.

So we experience it — when I might use this expression yet again — in this world historic moment, how the social question so blatantly, so tangibly insistent, approach from all sides by fanatics who see themselves sometimes as good practical people, who claim: 'We need people to back out of materialism, out of outer materialistic life to a certain spirituality, to a spiritual view of life.' They do not tire from quoting or making statements about personalities who in the past — the past has to be the rule, the present has less authority — had expressed certain ideal ways towards spirituality. Yes, you can have the experience that when someone points to something as practical and necessary as daily bread, it is pointed out that the primary importance is for people to return to the spirit. This warning contains unbelievably much of what had led mankind into the present catastrophe, fanaticism, which appear behind the most varied masks today and play a role in the facts. Certainly, on the one side it is fanaticism when someone, without being cognisant of outer practical living conditions, draws up some social ideal, called Utopian, and out of this finely fits and crystallizes a prescriptive system for living in order to be happy or satisfied or something or other. Basically, even when such Utopia appears full of criticism, it neither comes down to the criticism nor to good will, but it comes down to how they place themselves in practical life. Today it does not involve people being directed to a return to the spirit but that spirit exists in those who think about the social organism today. Today the importance is on the How, the Manner and Way in which thinking is arrived at. For my sake people don't talk about spirit but about the manner and way one talks about practical life, be it spiritual. Present time will be better served this way than through fanaticism reminding people in every third sentence to return to spirituality because usually those who are addressed can't imagine this spiritually, precisely because those who make these statements can't actually use imagination with which to present spiritually. The idealist utopians who insist — and these days they are not low in numbers — on finely thought-out social ideals are not the worst, because as a rule they don't hold water. One soon finds out these things are impractical and do not originate out of circumstances in real life.

Far worse are the masked fanatics in today's reality, who appear to be coming out of apparent practical life situations but these situations actually have to relation to reality but exist in lifeless abstraction. Still, we have fanaticism — one must always speak freely from the heart — we have experienced this in present events only too significantly. It is difficult to recognise it. It is difficult because we have not sharpened our gaze in this area.

Some people appear to have characteristics of fanatics — incidentally nothing at all should be said against the qualities of fanatics, they could be good people, they could be doing their duties in their field, could even be excellent people — but when the fact is stressed regarding the relationship some personalities have to fanaticism, then some people are quite astounded that these personalities can be associated with fanaticism because these fanatics appear to think with independent judgement, while these judgements are actually nothing other than wild superstition. I have for instance in the course of the last few years looked at some "life practitioners" — I say this in quotation marks — of fanaticism. With reference to this, if humanity wants to advance in knowledge it may experience some inner paradoxes. It will appear for example as a surprise, if I propose the most imminent *Ludendorff*, as a fanatic. The judgement of his supporters and his opponents go in quite different directions. The important thing about his personality is that with the exception of the field in which he is highly scholarly, namely strategy, he is in all the rest of his thinking adhered to abstraction, totally strange in life where his fanatical thoughts, which have no relation to reality, now take on power and result in unspeakable evil by his fanatical thoughts entering into reality. In this way, various personalities we know today and see as practical in life, could cause unending evil as typical representatives of fanaticism.

In the nineties of the nineteenth century fanatics appeared as if in an epidemic; coming from America they flooded Europe in the then so-called "Society for Ethic Culture." Here was an attempt at something having nothing to do with life, which could only come out of an abstract sensing of a certain ethic impulse and be propagated as ethical culture. If someone who was asked to do this, pointed out that such things harboured fanaticism, such things imprisoned and limited thought and thus made it impossiblc to discover the actual truth, they were either not understood or misunderstood or ridiculed.

This fanaticism should contrast itself with real truthful thinking which I believe has been represented through many years in the true spiritual scientific point of view. What actually is this spiritual scientific world view?

Essentially the spiritual scientific world view means it is not defined as a mere mirror image of observation of outer sensory reality but that it addresses spirit as coming from a real super-sensory experienced world, as real as what our eyes can see, ears can hear or touched by our hands. This viewpoint is less concerned with singular theories uttered about the actual spiritual world but rather far more involves everything experienced as knowledge coming out of the spiritual knowledge of the world and takes on an inner soul understanding into itself, an inner state in life through which the human being feels enlivened by soul spiritual beings in a real spiritual world. It is not dependant on what is said about the spiritual world but comes down to how people feel while in this spiritual world. It may already be that some or other super-sensible belief exists. This belief however, can just as easily steer towards fanaticism, like with those who strive towards goodwill. It comes down to this feeling: through the way one thinks, the way one experiences it, is within thinking, it flashes like lightening through one's own soul as the vital active spirit is experienced flashing through the soul.

This living, active spirit is in us. It is there like things outside are in space and events outside happen in time. When you take this expression in order to really spiritually acknowledge it not merely by thinking about it but living into it, then out of this spiritual acknowledgement an inner impulse arises, which is an incentive to make spirit something real out of itself, in the world; an incentive to experience the spirit as a reality and to make it a reality in quite a different way than what it can be as a mere mirror image of ideas and concepts which deals with the spiritual. There is a big difference whether one says: I think about the spirit, I believe in the spirit — or whether one says: Within me thinks the spirit, I experience the spirit within me. — The concept of ordinary faith actually loses its meaning through this experience. Coming out of this experience a soul-spiritual power will enter into the evolution of mankind. This soul-spiritual power which should enter into humanity's experiences is of a far greater importance than can be imagined, because it is the healing medicine for the laming type of ideology characterised here last week, which the proletariat inherited as a depressing element from the bourgeoisie.

This is what lives as the first true form of the social question in reality, if one penetrates this question in order to understand it in depth, that the development of modern spiritual life since the turn of this newer time during the 14th Century gradually became so blunt, weakened and paralysed that people didn't know any more that within them the spirit is alive as something real, full of life, but that they believe they only have ideas and mirror images containing some or other reality. These images they have in the world and which exist in the modern proletarian view of life is such that they say: 'The only thing that exists in the spiritual realm is ideology. Reality only exists in economy, in financial processes, in class conflicts — this is where reality exists.' However, something steams up in the human soul, it takes on the form of images of revelation, images which express science, morality, religion, art. This gives a superstructure based on a solid, real foundation. If one also can't admit to sociology living as an ideology in this superstructure being able to work back into the economic life, then it remains an ideology. No healing element comes out of this ideology if real spiritual participation, like spiritual science wanting to enter into modern humanity, is not engaged through spiritual experiences. Healing the damage in this ideology is only possible through real deepening in the real spirit and its manifestations, through deepening the real supersensible world. Everything which worked as spiritual life within the modern proletarians and was introduced as culture appeared as mere ideology and because ideology was seen as nothing, the soul was unable to experience a certain impetus, a certain momentum within consciousness which can be sensed in the higher sense, and souls were left dissatisfied and empty. Out of this soul emptiness developed the hopeless mood of the proletarian world view, where one part of it grew into a member of the real social question. As long as people will not realize that the tendency towards ideology needs to be healed and therefore are unable to introduce any positive impulses into the modern proletarian souls, so long will mere criticism remain in the modern proletarian regarding the developing capitalism, economic order and their world view.

This will not be accomplished without the will to enter a real practical view of life, a view of life which is not made up of theories or mere religious ideas, but with someone who wants to live, who wants to be creative, with a will to create individual impulses in life. For this some things are necessary and this scares today's individuals away as if it is something quite radical. What is intended here is far less radical than what comes out of life, provoked by modern instincts confronting people when they are too comfortable to turn towards what is necessary.

What I have been aiming at from a certain angle involves one member of the social organism which needs to develop out of modern living conditions as one of the three members, just as I have been sketching here last week, Wednesday. On that occasion, I dealt with the misfortune, in a certain sense, of modern humanity, when it is not examined — and it is so indeed, it is not being examined — that what should consist in a threefold way and that the three individual members work together in a lively way, has been turned through their power into chaos and a random organism which they want to continue to make so.

Now to not make myself misunderstood, I'm mentioning almost in parenthesis, my intention is not to advocate a complete reversal to be accomplished in a day. I'm giving indications in a certain direction towards which single questions may be orientated, questions about the state, spiritual life and economic life and how these meet in people's lives. There is no need to believe in things right away, as I present them; what we call 'the state' today can be made into something quite different tomorrow. People only need the will forces to relate to these things, to actualize the Christian "change your way," which means, the details, the individual measures presented need to be entered into if one wants to get their meaning, in order to orientate their configuration in a certain direction.

Thus, I have set out what people want to muddle together into a uniformed state just like one would try to do with the human organism — and make a Homunculus as a result — botched together to centralize the three systems in chaos so that the attempt at consolidating everything into a combined state enterprise forces the three living members apart rather than allowing a healthy social organism to develop. In one independent member within the social organism, all that relates to spiritual culture must develop; as a second independent member in the social organism everything related in the narrower sense to the political state life, not consolidated but in a lively exchange with spiritual life, need develop; and as a third independent member the economic organism. A spiritual organism, state organism, economic organism — of this people should be saying: in the next ten to twenty years evolutionary forces of humanity will be striving towards this. Whoever opposes this development is opposing the possibilities for progress in modern humanity.

The first point I want to touch on is from this view I'm considering today comprises the following: the life of so-called spiritual culture, all inclusive of what could be termed school and educational impulses, all that could be included in religious life, all that is artistic, literary and also all that relates to private and criminal law. These things I will still characterise more precisely. Everything decided in life regarding spiritual culture, positioned on a communal but independent basis, must be placed alongside the rest of the social organism. It must be placed by itself, it must be placed on such a basis that one can say: the vital element of this member of the social organism must have its centre in the free unfolding of the physical and spiritual arrangement of the human being. Everything needs to be based on this sphere of the individuality. Everything flowing into this must come from the centre of the human individuality and the physical and spiritual faculties must have free evolutionary possibilities but must however be withheld from influencing the remaining cultural life in some or other damaging or limiting or unreasonable way.

In this particular sphere, something can be achieved. I would like to offer a grotesque example. Please excuse me if this example appears grotesque but it will conceivably illustrate what I want to say. Let us take some or other young student, in other words a person budding within spiritual development, who has to deliver his doctorate. He obtains advice from authoritative personalities to edit some theme which has hardy or never been done before — let's take for example, dealing with the swear words of an old Roman writer. Such things really exist as those who are implicated with it, already know. Now the young man works for a whole year with these swear words of some ancient writer. Today one says: 'This is scientifically important.' — Well yes, from the side of this observation which exists in certain areas, it is certainly important, but now something else comes into consideration. It is the positioning of such a thing in the totality of the social organism. One needs to look away from the fact that it may well be interesting to write about swear words of some old writer. I know a dissertation where a young man was terribly plagued by the subject of parenthesis used by an old Greek writer.

I don't have anything that can be said against a pure scientific viewpoint presenting these things. Philistine details will not be made relevant here. However, in relation to it finding its position within the social organism the following is valid: the young man needs true diligence for possibly a year and so he needs to eat, drink and clothe himself. In order to do so he needs some income, capital. What does it mean to say: 'He consumes a certain amount of capital?' It means nothing other in the real life than: Many, many people must work for him.

What he eats, drinks, where he finds clothing, engages a whole army of people during these years. A small army is involved in his food, drink and clothing and this comes into consideration in relation to the social effects of the case. Today one mostly has the view that things can simply be taken thus, without a social understanding, out of a certain inclination to purely place these interests scientifically in the world. Our life in the present demands however that every branch in its relationship, in its vital connection to all the other of life's branches should be conceived with social understanding, with a feeling for the social aspect.

As I said, I've asked you to excuse me with this grotesque example; it could have been less grotesque but I chose this one in order to show you how necessary it is to develop a feeling for the social sphere, how spiritual life, the entire activity of the spiritual life need to stand within the social organism, in order to be justified in the general interest of humanity. The general interest of humanity may be asked whether the determination of swear words of some ancient writer has such worth that it requires a small army or workers to be appointed for an entire year. The question can of course be made less grotesque by working around it from other sides. One could then realize that spiritual culture can also include, for instance, the experience belonging to technical ideas and work in a lively way in other structures, in the rule of law for instance, because these things have a relative independence in life. Against this works centralization which steers everything into chaos.

Spiritual life must exist in a relative independent way, must not submit only to one's inner freedom but must stand within the social organism of one's spiritual life in order to position itself completely free of competition, resting on no state monopoly. That which is justified as a spiritual life — what this means for single individuals — is another thing. We are talking here about the social organism. Spiritual life is to be completely free of competition, completely free to meet singular needs of the community as they may reveal themselves. Someone might create poems, as many as he wants; may find friends for these poems, as many as he likes; what validates spiritual life is only what he, as a single individual, shares with other people. This is however only presented on a healthy basis when everything considered as spiritual life, everything from school to university life, everything from educational to artistic life need to be disrobed of any state monopolising characteristics and be contained by itself as independent

— but as we said, not from one day to the next. Direction is thus indicated for people placed on their own — this is how *the* bridge can be created towards something different. Due to a request, I have been occupied for some years during the nineties with my book "**The Philosophy of Freedom**" (later translation: '**The Philosophy of Spiritual Activity**') which has just been newly reprinted, perhaps in a favourable time, to show that a true experience of freedom cannot be said to be anything other than the actual play of the spiritual life into the human soul.

At that time, I called it the enactment of intuition in the human soul, the play of something totally spiritual. This real spiritual element must be born in the human soul in the light of freedom — free from competition — then it will live in a right way in the social organism. It may not — and this is important — be placed under some or other regulatory law of some or other branch of the social organism. It must be able to reveal itself in full freedom, as a result of general needs.

I know — and I will present this again in the following lectures — that many people think that if schools would be a free choice then we will be surrounded by illiterate people. I would like to show this will not be the case. Of importance today for me is to point out how, out of the inner nature of the thing, the necessity for a free spiritual life will be shown in the social organism. There are states where natural science, like nearly everywhere, is the monopoly; their enterprise is monopolised through the state which proclaims a law: 'Science and its education is free.' This however remains merely a phrase and will remain only a phrase if spiritual life does not persist in being held by itself. Not only may spiritual life, in relation to its activity in personalities, in relation to what is publicly said or dare not be said, depending on another member of the social organism when these other members instruct schools and universities, when I only mention it; not only, as said, the outer operation, the appointment of personalities, the limitations which may not be mentioned, become determined as a result, but that it also determines the inner content of spiritual life itself. Our whole scientific life has characteristics of political life, since in the more modern time the spheres of political life have spread over spiritual life. Spiritual life may however not be the affair of some or other member of the social organism; it can only uphold its self-contained content when this develops freely out of the human individuality.

Spiritual life stands opposite pure economic life just like the digestive system stands opposite the head system in the natural human organism. Economics has its own laws. The character of modern economic life has been identified through the proletarian science in an experiential, vital manner, not as a theoretical science preached from the rostrum but in order for it to become clear how proletarian science, just like economic life, relates to humanity in general.

Now one could refer once again to a certain point. I have mentioned this point in previous lectures. What is striking in economic life today, or with reference to the proletarian scientific consideration of economic life, is, and also in relation to it, the proletariat has been taken over by the inheritance from other classes. Whether it is through modern technology, whether through modern capitalism — as explored in previous weeks here — the human focus is as if hypnotized on economic life as the actual and only reality which can be linked to, in the social organism. People believe, when one talks about human evolution that only economic life needs to be referred to. We have seen how this economic life has become quite committed, how through economic life a particular active impulse in the bright light of the sun of human experience has moved the modern Proletariat's feeling of becoming human — this must be considered precisely, against economic life. The result of this is *Karl Marx*'s inflaming of millions upon millions of Proletarians that people believed he primarily, in clear language, pointed out to the Proletarians the worth of humanity in his entire statement: he, Karl Marx, first pointed out to the Proletariat that labour equals goods, labour could circulate as goods on the market and stand under the law of supply and demand.

Karl Marx used various erroneous ways to point out basic facts. That he referred to the innermost nerve of the modern social question anyhow, made his merits appear sufficient in the feelings of proletarian souls. Also here, social psychology has a far more reality based meaning than theories, observations, and discussions which are linked to some scientific and social life impulses. Out of this a vital question arises. How could the experience of human worth be conquered? That human labour is dealt with like goods? — This is what Marx had to say next. As we said, in many ways there are errors but this is not relevant now when an erroneous fact became so powerful in millions of human souls that it became a social fact. This is what Karl Marx said and this is how they understood the modern Proletariat. This understanding, while it has altered in some relationships, still work today, work particularly strongly in feelings. This is what he said: 'Within the economic organism goods are brought to the market and sold. There are owners of goods, prospective owners and buyers of goods. Between these exists the circulation of goods. The modern Proletarian has nothing other than his own labour. For each unit of goods, a certain production cost is necessary. The production of this or that product, until it is consumed, has this or that value. The modern Proletarian only has the power of his body, the only power he possesses is that of labour. In order to determine the production cost of labour all his needs to be included: his acquisition of nourishment, clothing and so on, and so the spent labour becomes replaced in turn. That is the production cost of his labour.' — Now, Karl Marx said, and in his inner being this also means the modern proletariat: 'Naturally the employer gives the employee no more than the so-called wages, without compulsion, for the work as the production cost for his labour. If however, the job continues for five hours and all the production costs are covered, the modern entrepreneur is not satisfied. He demands longer working hours. So the worker labours for free because he only earns as much as his "goods" — his labour — amounts to. What work he does additionally is added value. This is what he brings to the altar — if one could call it an altar — of capitalism, which collects as capital but actually originates from his labour, and as a result, because he is only paid the production costs, he is forced to offer his wares on the labour market, according to economic relationships, with all he has: his goods called "labour."'

You can with the greatest human ingenuity, applying the deepest national economic knowledge, discuss what can be done in the social organism that the worker should not carry his labour to the market as goods, that he can rid the world of this last result of slavery and you will, even by employing the greatest intelligence, the most profound national economic knowledge regarding many human lives, arrive at no solution. You will find no outcome to this question because the imminent sense of this question can't be discussed, can't be answered theoretically, but can only be answered through life itself, through creating something in life which strips away the characteristic of goods from labour.

If I might offer a comparison I would like to point to this little man in Goethe's Faust which Wagner produces as a test tube baby: Homunculus. It is made out of what human thoughts can imagine are ingredients from nature, but he does not become a person but remains a little manikin, a Homunculus. In the same way, you may combine something out of ingredients of understanding or out of national economic created ingredients — and your result will be a social Homunculus! Just as we need certain conditions in order to create a living human being, so in the same way, conditions need to be created towards a vital social organism which works progressively in life, not through theories, not through arguments. Human labour needs to be separated from the mere circulation of goods and may not be realized as such.

This will not be accomplished in any other way, if you look into it, in order for a social organism to be lively; it must have independent members, with the spiritual member beside the legal-state member, in a narrower sense the political-state member, and relatively independent beside that, the economic organism which lives under its own laws. Just as little as the stomach can breathe or direct the heartbeat, so little can the economic organism develop law out of its own forces. Economics will never develop its own laws when it works only from its own actual basis. Out of this actual basis the social organism will only be driven from production and commerce to consumption.

Just like the circulation of goods stand opposite nature itself, this foundation of all production, all consumption, all human events and so on, of profession and trade, so must on the other side stand in opposition, not determined by the economic organisation but that the economy determines, the existence of politics in the state's laws. This must be independent of the economic organism just like the lung-heart system is relatively independent of the head and nerve system.

Just because they work independently yet together, they have the right relationship in life. Only by the lungs and heart being isolated from the stomach, do they function relatively independently in the correct way together.

Only by there being in the lively social organism an independent member which does not determine on some or other economic grounds that labour becomes goods, but allows, out of the vitality of life for labour to be positioned in the social structure so that it becomes a right in the social structure, only through this, on the other side, can the economic life be allowed to be determined through the life or rights, the political life of the state in a narrower sense, as is determined by the natural foundation of economic life. Only then, when these three members exists side by side, when you have an independent spiritual member, an independent legal system member or actually state life plus an independent economic life and these members work in relative independence with one another, when each of these members out of its own foundation finds its representatives, its administrative body, we can say, its kingdom, its federal day, its ministry, and the single members are as sovereign among one another like single states who only trade through delegations, only then does the social organism really becomes healthy. Then the foundation of interest develops in the area of economics which is the only impulse crucial to the economic life. Then the question can be raised from life according to events taking place in other members of the social organism, in the legal organism: if out of the impulses of the legal body limitations are placed on human labour which from then on does not have the character of goods but the characteristics of rights, when labour flows into a specific economic branch where it does not pay, then this economic branch in relation to non-payment need be looked at, like when through a too expensive raw material it is not paid. This means that human labour becomes the dominant element in relation to economic life, not dominated, not enslaved. This is not accomplished by making certain laws but by creating a living body which must simply be something different than human impulses in a separated body, continuing from epoch to epoch snatching labour from the character of goods, because this character of goods must be torn out otherwise it will ever and again be absorbed because the economic body has the tendency to always suck up the capacity for work and make it goods only. The state body must be ever awake and remove the labour force from the stamp of goods.

Everywhere in life it appears that this muddling along — if I may use this trivial expression — makes the three social spheres a disaster. The social catastrophe which has taken place in the last four and a half years only needs to be considered. You can study the actual events. It is a lovely study for instance in the area in Austria which appears to have fallen apart into atoms: How has the inner structure actually held up, how has it wanted to hold since more than half a century? Here we have the so-called empire state. In this empire state a certain representation of nations exist, only in certain layers. This representation collapsed — not recently but where events prepared it, in the second half of the 19th Century — into four councils, the council of large landowners, of rural communities, of cities and markets and industrial areas, chambers of commerce; in other words, the rural communities, the cities, the industrial areas and the chambers of commerce. You see nothing about basic economic impulses existing in this representation. This representation was the representation of the state. This representation had laws. It only came from there because people were powerless under the influence of modern developments, as I've indicated under our consideration today, to penetrate economic life itself with their own organisation because their thoughts were too tightly meshed, too limiting because they could not plunge into them. People took the economic life as a frame for the rising state and bungled economic and state life with one another. Before people will not see that this bungling of innumerable causes has led to our present catastrophe, the sooner they will not go to ruin but towards a true cure.

Today I could once again only give a few indications. The day after tomorrow I will allow myself to expand the remarks. I want to still make another observation. Even in relation to the mighty world politics can what I said be substantiated, if you only want to go into the substrate of life. Whoever studies the Genesis of this terrible war, which is no war in the old sense but various ingredients of human catastrophes cooked up together which have not appeared at its end but entered at its crisis, whoever studies the Genesis of this catastrophe will find for instance that the importance of the starting point was totally directed towards the preparation and the expansion of modern economic life in a specific way and that this modern economic life, as a result, cannot be understood as being separated in the right way from a naturally and really vitally formed social organism, or in an organism found all over the world, because this economic life has been connected with the bare seven state laws which should have remained independent. As a result, essential economic factors and economic elements were there and they served the state power forces during the last decades, the economic powers which work in disharmony against one another. Were they held to develop merely on the foundation of their economic life and on the foundation of their common consensus it would never have led to this catastrophe. Towards this catastrophe they approached as purely economic forces while these economic forces had to serve as a false political entity of political powers of state whose armies were sent into the fields on their behalf.

These things need to be examined in a relevant way, not only theoretically. Some people do this of course. Still, one needs to know how to lift the actual impulse of the real social question, urgent and burning, into the light in a relative way into the present, in order to discover the real symptoms. Then you exit fanaticism as a mere warning and discover the reality within it, which makes it possible to allow the three members of the social organism to work together. What no discussion, no national economic judgement is able to do for economic and political life to exist side by side and so solve the labour force question, could continue to get rid of the most essential and difficult points in the modern proletarian's experience in the right way.

Now, the day after tomorrow I will continue with these observations, entering into detail in some of them which must remain as questions today, which will then be cleared up in a proper way. I just want to point out one thing. It has been and will be for a long time still, the comfortable thinking habits of people to find it radical, perhaps too academic in some or other way, what in truth is not some abstract idealism, but is actually everyday practical life. Some will say: 'Indeed, here comes a spiritual scientist who wants to by means of an imminent question, through a world historically important question, involve the social question.' Precisely not for something extraordinary for me or for the representatives of some conviction is what I'm validating here, so to say, but in relation to such people who take these things as impractical, a lost cause, while they don't look over the possibilities, can't envisage the perspectives. For these people, not for me, I would like to use a comparison at the closing today.

I would like to refer to some poor chap, *Stephenson*, who was condemned to sit at a 'Newcomenschen' steam engine (by Thomas Newcomen) and open and close the taps alternately, allowing steam out the one side and the entry of condensation water on the other. Now this little chap noticed up above, a balance swinging up and down and he thought: How would it be if I tied one tap to the other tap with a string, to the balance? Then at one moment the one tap will be opened and the other closed, and the next instance the one will close and the other open. The balance will do my work for me, I can only sit and look — so the little chap thought. And he actually did this. Now something could well happen as it is with many such things, when something quite new enters into life, for some quite clever person to then exclaim: 'You stupid young man, you must do as you are supposed to do! What kind of string have you tied to the balance? Remove it quickly or otherwise I'll tie you to it!'

It didn't happen quite like this but it is one the most important discoveries if the modern time, the automatic control of the steam engine which sprung out of the experience of this little chap. To have developed more insight towards only the self-control of a social organism which leads toward a vital interactive cooperation of the three members — its self-manipulation of spiritual members, legal-political member, economic member — to be more raised than this, spiritual science has no claim. It depends on whether all the clever people will say of this spiritual science: 'You stupid young man! Do your duty' or if you will look into what is actually happening. This must often be done if one is to be involved in all humility and without insolence. The belief in fanatics who label themselves as practical might soon give way to knowledge that the real practical people can be notorious idealists who could enter into the realities of life, that it could be them who may research the real evolutionary conditions of mankind and only through knowledge and the evolutionary process modern humanity could find the way which could lead to the solution of the social question — we will speak about this next time — that it is even possible in real life at all. Not via the route of presumptions by which many practitioners lay the law today, but probably the real-life practitioners, the clever idealists who can really penetrate the realities of life, have to prove it.

THE EVOLUTION OF SOCIAL THINKING AND WILLING AND LIFE'S CIRCUMSTANCES FOR CURRENT HUMANITY.

Lecture 4

by Rudolf Steiner

given at Zurich, 12 February 1919

wn.rsarchive.org/Lectures/GA328/English/eLib2017/19190212p01.html

Perhaps the lectures which I have been able to give here during this week and last week, proves from a certain point of view that it is justified to say that the situation of current humanity is deeply influenced by the developments which social thinking and social will have been adapting in the course of more recent times up to the present. More perhaps than most people suspect, the social impulse will penetrate directly into the life of single people — this penetration will happen more and more. It will become the determining factor towards the powers of the most individual behaviour. People are hardly able to understand their position within the human community which heaves and pulses with social impulses under examination, how its origins actually developed out of two different human shifts in the course of recent times — into social thinking and social willing. As a result, the continuation of these origins works into the present, works in such a way that it actually gives a social form to our current life.

I have mentioned in my lectures that solutions are not to be found towards understanding such things by doing what one usually does, by taking history as a straight line and regarding it as cause and effect in order to always reach a conclusion by what had gone just before. I have tried to draw attention to this: the historical life of humanity in its essence or foundations in relation to certain crises in the course of events, or rather better said: of the presence of crises during the course of events — are similar to what happens in the life of individual people. In the life of individual human beings there is no straight line of development; results arrive without a leap out of what went before. It is necessary to take the comfortable but often misunderstood conception that nature makes no leaps in a corresponding way by observing time and again how in the course of an individual life, crises appear, like the crisis in the sixth or seventh year of life with the change of teeth, how these crises arrive out of elementary organic foundations, just as it similarly rises to puberty. Whoever has knowledge of the course of human life can show how such critical changes also appear later in life even if they are not taken in as decisive a way by superficial observation as the first two. To observe such critical changes in the course of life is necessary in order to really understand the history of life. As much as current humanity is averse to such observation and listening, just as necessary is it right now to promote the social understanding of life and to point out such things with radical intensity. One of the last big changes — this I explored in the previous lectures — in the course of evolution of mankind we can point out as having taken place at the turn of the 15th, 16th Centuries. Only if one does not enter deeply enough into the historical course of things will one not know how radically different everything is which happens in the human soul as demands, as desires demanding certain satisfaction; how that changes in relation to what had arrived before that moment.

Now at the same time, as if followed by this elementary change in the later times of man's evolution, something appears which can be expressed as follows: the social impulse lived within the human soul in earlier times; this social impulse led to the structure of the social impulse. In earlier times, this social impulse was experienced instinctively. People lived together socially, ordered their affairs socially within their community. At that time, in the place of instinctive thinking and willing, a change started to take place towards a more conscious social impulse. This conscious impulse came to the fore gradually and slowly but it distinguished itself by shifting modern humanity radically away from the situation of medieval and ancient humanity. Here we see immediately how with the taking up of the social impulse out of the instinctive and into the conscious life, clearly two streams are created, indicating two diverging movements of social thinking and willing.

The one stream is clear in those people who can still up to today be called the foremost, leading social class of humanity. The other stream appeared somewhat later but is clearly distinguishable from the former, which we today describe as the Proletarian world. The leading intellectual bourgeois circles with all their interests as modern time came along, are linked to all that was created as the newer state which had gradually developed out of the structures of medieval community life. These bourgeois leading circles are through their interests linked to what we have placed under the three members I have explored as the social organism, describable as the actual constitutional state, as actually politically constituted, whether instinctive or consciously based regarding the relationships of one person to another. As with ancient traditions and also with a certain reference to newer scientific relationships, the leading bourgeois circles linked their interests more or less to what many people held as the only social form, namely the state. As a result of them moving consciously from the old instinctive social life to the modern consciousness, they thought as a result of anything related to the state were to be in terms of the constitutional state. As modern economic life became ever more complicated which through the expansion of the human horizon of activities became ever more complicated right over the world, so the leading circles tried to establish it in the structure of the state. They wanted to make the state ever more into the economist. This endeavour took on a certain course and we see that within certain circles single economic sectors were gradually drawn into the state structure. I pointed out such economic sectors last time. The essential aspect from this view is that social thinking earned quite a particular form as a result, in these circles, because of it wanting to conquer the state's interests: the encroaching complicated economic life.

The social impulse developed in quite a different way in the Proletarians. Now with the awakening in newer times the modern Proletarians didn't involve themselves as much within the real state territory. Due to a lack of time I can't enter into this further through deeper examination — but in their relationship, they stood quite removed from the interests of the leading circles and their representation in the state's structure. Still, the Proletarians were driven into the structure of the economic life in the most radical way. Their entire thinking and feeling unfolded in such a way that it was like a mirror image of what was being experienced in the economic life. Thus, the social impulse of the Proletarians became determined by the social structure of the economy of humanity, the economic life, just like the social impulse of the leading bourgeois and intellectual circles became determined by impulses of the constitutional state, by the impulses of the actual political structures. With both streams, they developed more and more in such a way that even these days there appears what I referred to in my lecture the day before yesterday, a gap, an abyss between the specific configuration of social thinking and feeling of leading bourgeois and Proletarian circles. I consider this to be the most tragic arrangement of mankind's situation in present times, the existence of this abyss which makes it so difficult for an understanding, to find a mutual understanding between both the two mentioned social classes. So it must come about as we will see: how prepared both the classes are in their struggle for existence in confrontation. The essential fact in this fight, which has partly already happened, is partly still being prepared, and that which can make sense, even still today only grasp community life superficially, will take on gigantic forms which are essential in order for, on the one side the bourgeois leading circles want the economy to become gradually captured by the state, co-capturing the state economy in such an extraordinary way which is the productivity and labour of the Proletarians themselves, and on the other side that the Proletarians want to conquer from the state the element where their interests are experienced in an isolated economic life.

That is the essential basic principle of this struggle which plays with so much meaning into the current situation of humanity. Over and beyond all that, as is often the case in awareness, it has been forgotten to pay attention calmly — I would like to call it, to what has been pushed down into the subconscious which lies behind the two impulses I've mentioned — to what is actually hidden. What wants to work on the surface of human lives since the critical change in the 15th Century entered later mankind, while what sweeps and drifts and pulsates in human life frequently only takes place in disguise in the consciousness: this striving towards an affirmation of the human personality appears which had not been known in earlier times. Assertion of the human personality, experiencing human nature within, actually makes up the nerve of the social question and dresses itself only according to the various relationships already determined by the given forms. So it could happen that this struggle towards the achievement of the complete assertion of all individuals, can become a struggle for all people — a struggle having become one of differing mutual interests, a struggle of the classes, a struggle which throws its forces in a disastrous way into the present.

Because this indicates something hidden and masked in the newer development of humanity it has resulted in focus not being directed, or better said, that people up to now have not learnt to direct their focus on what matters. During the time when the social impulse worked instinctively, people could allow the social organism to form itself instinctively. Because the social impulse has entered consciousness, even if in masked form, it is necessary right there, necessary as the most important thing in relation to the social problem of the more newer times, that social understanding, an understanding for the expression of the social organism in each individual enters, but that this understanding brings no learned aspect with it but brings an experience which lives in feelings and expresses itself in individuals as this or that necessity to situate themselves in the human community. For this reason, it is so necessary to do what I'm trying to accomplish in these lectures: to turn our focus on to the totality of striving in newer humanity which can only now penetrate the surface in a particular relationship, to focus on really making the social organism into a living form, a form which will allow humanity in their current situation to understand it in a lively way, not just in theory. For this reason, I point out that the health of the social organism depends on not making a chaotic jumble but that the three members are as follows: spiritual life in the widest sense, legal- or political life which means state life in a narrower sense and lastly, the economic life. Only in this way can those within the three members experience their necessary liberation, so that one of the three forms are not engulfed by one of the others but that they unfold freely beside one another and already in a certain independence as I have depicted from different viewpoints, now work together side by side. Up to now certain preconditions directed actual tendencies of human evolution against this independence. By differentiating what had been interwoven previously has now become the most needed current question in relation to the social nature of current humanity.

By exploring certain sides of human thinking, you can feel what I mean, that even in the light of consciousness the social impulse starts according to spiritual presuppositions respectively and they think in this or that way about the relationships between the life of the state and that of the economy. So we see the so-called social or national economics — whatever you want to call it, it is the same thing — formed out of ways of thinking, habits of thinking. It is not my purpose to present the social thinking of the newer time. I only want to draw your attention to one thing — actually I would like to shed light on several things which must be addressed in these lectures. Among these various ways of thinking, ways of presenting the interweaving of economic with state- and spiritual life, there appears also in this newer time what was designated in the 18thCentury as the so-called physiocratic national economic ideas. Earlier thinking had the intention of organizing economic life out of the state organism and this formed itself as by necessity in opposition against the physiocratic thinking. It was developing in such a way that there was a need to change economic life not being tyrannized by the state in a narrow sense, that economic life be responsible for its own natural laws, wanting it to be left to what it would fall into if humanity freely, simply out of his own interests guide the economic life. Experts had various revealing things to say which can be somewhat echoed. These people asked: What kind of system of laws should actually go into this form of political state which will regulate economic life? Either the laws are to be the same as those which economic life gives when it is left to freely play with the forces, or it will let others impose on it. If it is the first case, when it is the same, then it is not necessary, the others are not needed and economic life develops its own laws, particularly state laws do not need involvement in economic life. If, however, the state laws work against the economic life then it restricts it, it impairs it and can do damage to itself.

I would like to say that what is expressed in these two opposing statements still haunts many people's thoughts. It haunts them because modern humanity, even though they consider themselves very practical and have a sense for what is real, are still terribly consumed by a certain sense for abstraction, for theoretical one sidedness. Should one try to prove in how many people today what appears as practical life is none other than an actualized one-sidedness, realized one sided theory, then one will touch on some riddles of life and be able to find partial solutions. What sounds the most plausible, most independent for me is to say: Either state laws take on the same direction as the economic ones then they are not necessary, or you contradict them and by so doing, damage the economy. One thinks about these opposites only when one considers the social organism as something which allows itself to be regulated according to concepts, laws, principles and programs, when one does not face up to the social organism being something which has to have life, which must live through its own being. Whatever has come through its own content of life, through its own thriving and sprouting impulses of life, has in real life an opposition to it. The social organism, in order to be a reality, must have oppositions within itself.

For this reason it is necessary to express something which probably many theoretically orientated souls in current times will see as absurd: the state-, pure legal-, and pure political-life needs to be limited in a certain way, in its laws it needs to counteract the economic life in order for the community life of humanity not to be only an economic, not only a legal life situation but an economic, legal and spiritual one, so that it can unfold as we have seen in the example of the human organism. I will once again use this example — I don't want to play the game of analogy between physiology and sociology — the processes of the digestive system is in a certain way independent of those in the rhythmic system, breathing and heart system, both are limited and mutually restrained in their vital processes. So it is necessary that the placing beside one another within the real social organism is the economic life on the one side and in a narrower sense the state life on the other side, which must be joined by the relatively independent spiritual life, as I have illustrated last time from another point of view.

From the following we see what it's really all about. Economic life has quite different inner forces than the legal life, which have to work together if the totality of life is to prosper and this is different again with spiritual life. You could, if you wanted to bring something more or less concretely lively into abstract forms, even if from a one-sided view in order to make it understandable, say the following: in economic life, as in the production of goods, circulation and consumerism, it all comes down to a corresponding creation of value. This creation of value is accomplished essentially by value building itself if the social organism is to be healthy, under the influences and impulses, that the consumption for which the economic organism takes responsibility — call it market or something else — has it ready for consumption so that the consumer of the goods benefits as far as possible. Goods must be offered for consumption if the social organism is healthy, in such a way that it is completely used in an expedient way, that it lasts for as long as it is useful, or for as quickly as it can be consumed while it is useful, that in any case its entire content depends on consumption.

If human labour would be so totally engaged in economic life — and this economic life can only develop in the healthy way under the historical points of goods-price development according to the corresponding consumption — so what the Proletarians with Marxist viewpoints had hoped for, would be fulfilled, human labour being considered as goods. In this way human labour becomes tainted with the characteristics of goods in the social organism, because it is being considered in its ability to be fully utilised for its worth.

The economic member of the social organism also has, when looked at more closely, the tendency to use people and should the economic member of the social organism only follow its own rules, then human labour would be used up. Because the leading bourgeois circles do not take this into account, they have contributed to the situation that within economic life and the position of the Proletariat in economic life, the very nerve of the modern social question has developed, indicating that the life of the modern Proletariat shows, particularly for himself, he chose to undress his labour of the character of goods. As it is sometimes masked in the social question and much of it living unconsciously in the Proletariat, it is the important element which the Proletarian soul strives for, the liberation of human labour from the character of goods.

This can never happen if the economic processes follow their own laws and when the totality of state life is only made into a single economy as is the ideal of many modern socialists. This can also not happen when in a one-sided way the state out of itself is made into an economist. A healthy relationship can only come about if the economic organism can be allowed to unfold its relative processes by itself, when, as it happens in natural organic life as well, a system is allowed to gradually develop fully out of its own latent forces, is allowed to unfold in relative independence. Whatever arises out of this unfolding and is being limited, becomes changed by an adjacent relatively independent system, just like it happens in a natural organism having developed its system fully, which also only expresses its harm as these losses are continuously being paralyzed by the adjacent system. All organic processes are based on this. On this the healing of the social organism must also be based.

It really doesn't matter to me how the economic organism is defined, how one thinks about it. For me it matters that these two branches need to be side by side and that they each develop independently even with the predisposition of developing damage within, so that the other system adjacent to it develops and paralyzes that which arise as damage in the other system. That is the nature of what is alive; that is also what the nature of a living social organism need to be. Only when the economic body manages itself on its own terms and the legal and political bodies manage themselves, whether along their own terms which result from the regulation or the legal relationships between people; when these organisms regulate themselves independently because they are working side by side and on each other, then a healthy social life will be formed. The social question will not be solved through theories, not solved by laws but it will be solved through there being in actual life the forces, one kind being the economic, beside the others, the stately, the political, working directly in their own existence, that they both work adjacent to one another and develop in one another, but by developing in such a way that each one maintains its independence.

This has been missed, out of a certain historical necessity. What has happened has of course been necessary. No criticism but a formulation of relationships is to be presented here. This needs to be taken as essential today if human progress is to orientate itself now and towards the future. It is a given that for the sake of the recovery of the social organism, economic life will become an associate, and becomes divided in such a way that the cooperative societies, trade unions and so on are formed by stripping off what had been inherited from the prejudice of how a constitutional state should be formed. What still existed in state life within these associations has to be stripped off. They must become purely economic serving entities which are based on the relationship of the human being in the economic life, whether it is for the foundation of economic life, or whether it is for the necessity of adding value to raw materials, or to bring goods into circulation, the relationship of consumerism in the right relation to production and trade and so on. The complexity of human life makes it necessary today for the entire system of associations and coalitions which are created on the foundations of the economic life, to be formed through human beings; such associations and coalitions which essentially exist on the understanding of the exploitation of the foundations and the directing of goods towards appropriate consumption. Even the complexity demands the creation of an entire system of associations in this sphere. However, these associations would be designed out of the connection of people with economic powers themselves. The result could be something which again and again enters into real life which is the tendency of the economic life to use individuals.

Beside the economic life the political life must stand, which in contrast to the economic life, is founded on associations which must be based more on democracy because the state life encompasses relationships between people. It encompasses everything in which all people are equally interested in. As the economic life is based on the economic value of goods, so state life has to be based essentially on public law; based on law or with law as its foundation, which determines the relationships of one person to another. In a lively exchange in the economic life a restriction and limitation would have to take place. Approaches to this are available but a penetrating social insight must take place. Whatever is to be created must prioritise the protection of the human being from the economic orientation of consumption, also in relation to his labour being consumed.

Just as the creation of prices and values are the essentials within the economic body, so the arrangement of actual laws, of practical public laws regulating relations of one person to another, are essential in life of the political state. Can it not be said even today that in relation to the experience of public law, no particular clarity has been reached? Many questions can be raised to those who should know these things, who should have done research about these things which are actually to be understood under the essence of laws, laws which always appear in practical form. One only comes to an understanding of the difficulties when one looks for instance at the example of such questions raised in the doctoral dissertation of my friend who has passed away, *Ludwig Laistner* in his "The Right to Punish," This in itself can become a question which considers the actual right of the human community in relation to punishment.

One can try all kinds of ways to come closer to the impulse of the law. Particularly in our time when so much is being discussed from the most various sides about the law, it is obvious that to come ever closer, is to essentially search for the being of Law. If you try and find what lies behind such real Law -ownership is also based on law; the relationship of ownership being a piece of land or anything exclusive to one person, for his use with the exclusion of others — you find it is the subject of the actual political member of the social body and so you find nothing other than that it finally comes back to power. Others discover it actually goes back to an original human experience. One arrives far too easily at empty forms if you try to tackle it. Without me getting entangled — and this could involve hours of time — in a complete substantiation, I would still like to say that the law bases a certain relationship of people to something, to a thing, a cause or something similar, or a collection of causes, with the exclusion of other people. What is its basis then actually, if one can develop the feeling that someone or other or a nation has the right to something they lay their eyes on? Still, when one takes the pains, you come to say nothing other than legal rights are based on public life enabling an evolution for the activity of something or its causes or collection of causes which most probably do more for general humanity than any other. The moment one has the experience that someone has a relationship to something, or to someone else, where the need to general humanity is obvious, one can apply the relevant law for it. This will also be essential which will bring about the decisive factor through human experience when the big legal questions of international life now steps into the real world. One would fully award rights over a certain territory, to those who have the intention that in the sense of wellbeing of general humanity this nation in particular will be the best at making the territory the most productive.

So one comes to the impulse which can weave and flow through the democratic common wealth which must orientate the exchanges of one person to another, be it in workers' insurance or be it in other insurance, instituted to give protection against damaging economic life; in all of this human life lies as the foundation of law which I've just been speaking about. An understanding, but not an understanding for some or other general abstract definition of law, but an understanding for the effectiveness of the law, in every single real case, needs to enter to make it a healthy social life for humanity. This legal life, this life of the political state in a narrower sense, of the second member of a healthy social organism, that it will also be; the real crossing point, I would say, of the modern social question only, would not be through some realization of theories, principles and programs, but through direct life, created in the world, namely the point which I have referred to as the demand of the modern Proletarians: disrobing the power of human labour from being dressed up as goods.

To that end it is necessary for people to also really understand, I could say, understand out of the very foundation, what is involved in the share of human labour in general life, in the structure of the community. Again, it will involve hours to take this into consideration if I would attempt establishing one basic social law for human labour: intuitively and instinctively, I believe, every person can do it if life is penetrated fairly and comprehended regarding what I now want to express.

In my Newspaper called "Lucifer Gnosis" I tried to point out this fundamental social law in my contribution about the social question, which was published already at the beginning of the century. However, people were sermonizing about many things on this subject and even today, it falls to deaf ears, unfortunately. This law implies that no one, in as far as he or she belongs to the social body, the social organism, actually works for himself or herself. Just think, insofar as a person belongs to the social organism, he does not work for himself. Each act of work which a person performs can never fall back on him, also not in his actual yield, because it can only be performed for others. What other people produce must be good for us. It is not merely an ethical form of altruism which lives in these things, but a simple social law. We can't do it any other way, just as we can't redirect our blood, so the circulation of the human manipulation will work in such a way that our activity towards everyone and all the activities of others are to our benefit; our own work never reverts back on us.

However paradoxical it sounds, when you examine the real circulatory process in human labour within the social organism you will find the following: it originates in people and benefits others. What one side receives out of the labour is the result of the labour of the other side. As I said, as paradoxical it might sound, it is true. One person can just as little live from his own labour in the social organism as one can eat oneself to get nourishment.

Even though basically this law is easy to understand, you could argue: 'When I am a tailor and among the clothes I make for others, I also make myself a garment, then surely I'm directing my labour back on to myself!' — That is only an illusion as it is always a deception to believe that the result of labour falls back on oneself. By me making a skirt, pants or equivalent, I don't in truth work for myself but put myself into the position to work for others. This is the pure function human labour has in a social law within the social organism. Whoever dispels this law, works against the social organism. One works against the social organism when one implements the idea which has come about in the more recent history that the proletarian worker must live from the proceeds of his labour. That holds no truth, it is hidden through social relation means an achieved untruth, which penetrates and damages economic life. This can only be regulated in the economic life when the economic life has developed independently beside the relatively independent political-, narrower state life, which all the time snatches from the economic life, the possibility to link human labour back to itself. Within the legal system this is processed in the right social understanding where human labour retains the function it must get according to the truthful course of life in the social organism. The economic organism always has the tendency to use up the force of human labour. Judicial life must always refer to the natural altruistic position of labour and it is always, ever and again necessary, that through new concrete democratic legalization, what the economic life wants to accomplish in error, is to once again tear human labour out of the fangs of economic life on the way to public law. Just as the digestive system and the breathing-circulatory systems must work together, and the circulation of the blood absorb what the digestive system has absorbed, so there must be cooperation, a mutual interaction of what is taking place in the economic life and in the legal life, otherwise neither the one nor the other will thrive. The mere legal state, when it wants to become economic, paralyzes the economic life;

the economic organism, when it wants to conquer the state, kills the system of public laws.

This is what I wanted to add to what had been said in previous lectures towards the foundation of the Threefoldness of the social organism. Because the bourgeois leading circles have had their gaze hypnotized by the state, it has become something like a god to them. Focus is not being orientated towards the necessary differentiation of the social organism into three members. So it has come about in our newer times that the state has absorbed political life and in a narrower sense spiritual life. Just like the circulation of goods depends on price and wealth creation, like life within the political social organism depends on the legal life, so everything which is the spiritual life comes out of the direct content of the produce. Just think how enormous the difference is between economic life and spiritual life. In economic life, everything depends on goods being brought to a goal orientated use. Anything generated out of the spirit, be it in the sphere of education, schooling, be it in the sphere of art, or in some or other spiritual sphere, placing spiritual creativity in relation to its usefulness is quite an absurdity. It can't be done. What is brought about spiritually can't be placed on the same line as the circulation of the economic process. This has resulted in the absorption of the school system by the state, the university system and whatever similar by the state, which in the modern development is becoming a limiting factor, even in the real sense it is becoming a limiting factor. People need to become aware once again of making spiritual life free, unharnessed. I have already pointed out that something else needs to be added to the spiritual member of the social organism even though it appears as a paradox, and that is the actual practice of private and criminal judgement. As extraordinary as it sounds, there are tendencies in modern life also which are not judged in the correct way. What is increasingly taken into account in court through misguided psychology is the tendency towards, not an acknowledged, but need for acknowledgement of the principle of incorporating private and criminal processes in the spiritual member which exists relatively independently, and relates relatively independently to all in life which develops as the closer political life, which was developed out of pubic rights legislation. Certainly in future it will happen in a healthy social organism that a criminal for instance will look for results in the second, political member. If it however is looked for then he would be brought to trial by a judge who he will confront in an individual human relationship.

Regarding this question perhaps only those can judge from history, those like me, who is speaking to you now, who during years and years of observing a region where it has become really difficult to actually govern, and where one could still, I may say, want to be ruled through constraint according to a uniform state: in a region such as Austria. Here one can see what happened if across purely language boundaries a free jurisdiction should have been there; when despite the language barriers of those bohemians living in a German region near neighbouring Czech or Bohemian residents with bohemian judges over there, the bohemian residents could turn and choose their judges from the German region. You can see how beneficial this principle could work which unfortunately was only in the beginning of the aspirations in various school associations. Here is something, I might say, like a difficult nightmare still today, for those who have participated in Austrian life, which presses on the soul that this egg of Columbus has not been found: the free choice of a judge and the lively cooperation of the plaintiffs, of the judges and of the defendants, instead of judges presented out of the centralised political state, who can only be authoritative, not for the jurisdiction but for the visiting and delivering of the criminal or then for the delivery of the judgement.

As paradoxical it might sound today, the relationship of people to their judge in connection with criminal and private law must be incorporated in the independent spiritual member. Already two days ago I made you aware how it doesn't depend on an outer management as to the choice of persons in the spiritual branch of the state. If you look into modern relationships then you will see this as well, that the innermost life of science, art and everything spiritual is above all becoming dependent on what they should not becoming dependent on if the spiritual member is to develop relative independence beside the other members. It still appears like a paradox today when I say in conclusion that each of these areas must have a certain sovereignty, its own system of representation, its own legislation, developed out of its relationships, developed out of relationships of associations in economic areas, and so have its management, its legislation as independent. In a democratic way, there will develop out of the whole of mankind a particular social sphere for the actual political state in which the relationship of one person to another is regulated, as will be the relationship to economy and the relationship to spiritual life; without these two being interfered with by the state laws and as a result the spiritual life's active forces will give the layout for the management of spiritual life as well. To an even higher degree, the spiritual life can be emancipated from modern life, to a higher degree than it had been in olden times when the only spiritual life, which applied to many people, came out of religious life, out of schools and universities.

Certainly the intervention of the modern state was necessary to rebuke the antiquated forms of religion and obsolete management which suited them no longer. Out of modern life itself an independent spiritual life is to be developed. This is exactly why a spiritual scientific direction, the very foundation of this, needs to be taken into consideration on this basis because it is known that the entire actual productive spiritual life also lives in, for instance, technical participation, technically experienced ideas which can only develop with healthy human impulses, when it is developed out of the vital, autonomous spirit, independent from both the other members of the social organism. The human spirit will only acquire impact of productivity in the right way if spiritual life is relatively autonomous. Brooding, theorizing, inventing thoughts, for my sake as well, can also be experienced as it takes a certain direction in more modern technology and science, observable in their admirable methods, but the real productive idea, which is so productive that true human progress and at the same time real human healing is served, these ideas can only be born within a self-supporting, self-determining spiritual life.

As much as people are still alienated from what I'm actually implying which must be understood in order to place the social question on a healthy basis, some people have responded to what I've explained by saying: 'Yes, this is only a more modern meaning of the renewal of the old platonic idea of dividing the social body into three classes: the rulers/guardians, the fighters/auxiliaries and the producers/labourers/educational state.' No, this is no renewal of old platonic ideas but is in a specific relationship as the extreme opposite, if it comes down to it — because between the platonic thoughts considered great in Greece and also later times, and the thoughts of today towards a healing of the Social organism, lies the big, critical historic incision of the fifteenth Century. At the time of Plato, the divisions of the social organism was one of the division of classes. The structure which I'm talking about here was not a division of people but was formed by members of the social organism; this social organism was so structured that in some cases one person could belong to all three divisions of members, it was not damaging to move from one to the other, not even when, as in modern parliaments it often happens, the same person is accounted for as a farmer and at the same time belong to a party of the state. Today it is still possible through some or other association inaugurating an advocacy group, that an economic protection of interest can be passed through into law. Last time I mentioned such an example where an entire state's life of law was penetrated by such a protection of interests. This becomes excluded. However, my presentation of the threefold healthy social organism, excludes people from the social organism. People just become independent through it; they are stripped of the character of being slaves of the organism, where not classes of people, layers of people exist as members but that the social organism finds its own divisions. This points at the same time to these thoughts which form the basis of it, which should be taken from true reality, distanced from everything which I indicated as fanatical the day before yesterday.

This fanaticism appears in the most varied parties. It is even present in bourgeois circles on the side of social democracy. This fanaticism gets a hold on people if they don't gradually get an inkling of what the social organism as such can actually aim for, when it is healthy. Again and again, the social thinking suffers under the influence of the feeling, the idea, as if the social order can be aimed for directly through some or other program in order to bring good fortune or satisfaction to humanity, or something of this sort. This cannot be sought for directly. What can be aimed for directly is a social organism capable of life, one which has vital forces of life within itself. Situated in such an organism, living in such an organism can out of quite different foundations bring happiness to people. That has other foundations. However, these foundations need to be freed from being restrained. They can only be freed if the social organism is based on life giving forces. Just like a really viable organism can be of help to develop the soul, so in a comparative way can a viable social organism develop happy, satisfied human beings who are willing to work and have an understanding about work. This is what a healthy social organism is all about.

An observation of what we have experienced during a catastrophic time, one might say, can also be considered from an international viewpoint and corroborated out of a larger historic viewpoint, how these ideas I have been exploring as three members, are really necessary for the present-day form of life for humanity and also a form of life for humanity in the foreseeable future. One could say that before this terrible catastrophe, called a war, which broke out over humanity, there was a culmination of the thorough tossing and complete turmoil of the three members which should have reached a differentiation. Precisely due to these three members not being able to reach relative independence beside one another, the result has been much penetrating into what in reality must be calculated as the point of origin and the causes of these tragedies of war. Only a few details need to be pointed out. The focus of humanity has been entirely directed toward the idea that the war has its point of origin in the relation of the Austrian state with the Balkan, namely the Serbian relationship. Whoever was initiated into the Austrian relationships of the last decades know how to judge the economic connections taking place between Austria and the south-eastern Europe, and how these were being convoluted in an unnatural way in the relationships which were to have developed independently with the purely political. As a result of this amalgamation suddenly the political relationship could for itself decide about something which was deeply rooted in economic relations and as a result actualize a falsehood and explode.

How different these things could have been — I can only indicate a few things in my lecture today, in conclusion — if the relationships of such neighbouring states could have been representing the Threefoldness, when across the border the relationship could have been purely politically, democratically based and separated from the other members, just as the form of government is as usual. When however, the corrected, harmonized independently economic and spiritual factors work on the other side of the border, then the system of the state, the so-called state, would be propagated through interests in harmony and amalgamation, where the one is always correcting the other, where no one single side by itself can circumvent an explosion. Healthy relationships across borders would develop in international relationship of nations through Threefoldness.

And then again, how global mankind turned their eyes on what was happening in Germany at least outwardly, at the declaration of war. Whoever is initiated in this area knows how the disaster happened. Often it has been said that during July and August, in those fatal days, politics, beside the actual warfare, alongside the army, had failed. Politics and armies are there where they both work, running simultaneously. They are not divisible anyhow. They could only unfold in a healthy way, if they worked within one of the state formed three-fold social organisms. Otherwise politics would necessarily, at least in one member, take on a uniformed characteristic. At a given moment it would either culminate into the military or non-military. What has to be uniform through its very nature, even when it has been amalgamated through human error with other systems, it cannot do externally so that the one goes over to correcting the other. During these terrifying fearful conditions which grew out of Berlin during the last days of July and the first days of August, the process of coagulation into one single system took place, a system which should have been split up. They all became concentrated and responsible to one system which no single system for the healing of mankind had ever dared take on. Actual relationships would then clearly teach us if these things are investigated without prejudice and bias. Oh, how much nonsense is being said in relation to politics and the army! So much nonsense has been uttered in the last four and a half years! I only want to say one thing: if within an inseparable member of the social organism the dormant policies and strategy could only work, then never, when the strategy is led to depend on itself, will the policies influence this strategy in a healthy way. There has been a tendency to time and again refer to the clause of (Major General Carl von) Clausewitz (1780–1831): "War is a mere continuation of politics by other means," (Die Kriegführung sei die Fortsetzung der Politik mit anderen Mitteln).

I don't want to offer criticism about this statement in as far as it relates to the entire war analysis. However, just like men have, again and again — and women have done so as well — referred to this saying, it has just about as much sense as if one would say: "Divorce is the continuation of marriage through other means."

This kind of nonsense springs from unnatural thinking, which multiply and penetrate in an unnatural way into real relationships. When things are for once considered without prejudice then it will be apparent how differently things could have gone. Understandably what has happened is historically necessary and what must be said should be a valid impulse for the future, but hypothetically one could still say that everything could have happened differently if the structure of the international European relationships could have been under the influence of the social Threefoldness. One could then say: what has happened came through the relations of alliance. However, alliance relationships could never have entered under the influence of a Threefoldness. Such alliance training which these were and which led to the catastrophes of the last four and a half years, would be ended if people orientated themselves in the sense of the Threefoldness of a healthy social organism.

What I am opening up here has been thoroughly thought through with real meaning, it is brought out of thoughts from reality. I have also always said that if I had involved myself during these fearful years, an authoritative position corresponding to that time would have been to point out the Threefoldness: The only reality is that things change from one day to the next and understandably relationships could have changed regarding these things which need to be talked about. I say to people: 'What is presented here is no program, it is not an ideal; it corresponds to observations which want to be realized in Central and Eastern Europe, above all in Europe. You have the choice to either apply good sense today or to go and encounter revolutions and cataclysms.'

They have started already and will show themselves in other ways. Today however I might repeat a consideration which can be said on this occasion. I have always said: 'Whoever is a Utopian, a theorist, who does not think from the basis of reality, but out of abstract claims or party impulses, is interested in what a program or something similar can offer, and that this is actually executed according to specific details.' These things do not matter in what I am presenting — I have mentioned this before. It could be said — and still is said today — that the formulation of what I am representing will leave no single stone standing on another. The important thing is not that some or other conjecture is realised but that reality is tackled at some point. If this is done it will be discovered that through tackling it, the way forward will become clear. It could become clear by carrying it out and then all formulations need to be adjusted. This is not important if one is no Utopian, no fanatic, to execute something word for word, but to start it at a certain point. At such a point as to where it must start, I want to point out still today, before it becomes too late, before human instincts are so far unleashed that an understanding among people, perhaps decades from now, would not be possible any more.

In closing today, I still want to mention something — although in a narrower sense it doesn't belong to this lecture — I also think that if anyone feels within his soul that he is somehow connected to the social question, he has the task to not only speak up about it but need to apply all means to allow his understanding to be brought to his contemporaries. This is what we can do first: promoting mutual social understanding. Much has been corrupted, spoiled in the most varied areas throughout the world due to fragmented, mashed thinking, as I have characterised, resulting in disabling the right idea to come forward at the right time. As a result, I must greet the possibility with a certain satisfaction that out of the difficult relationships of the present it has become possible to accomplish practical results of ideas suggested here, in a relatively short time. Those individualities who have in a certain way, I could call it, been ignited regarding the social question with a view based on reality, have allowed themselves to work towards an understanding of these things, at least in these areas where today misfortune can be the biggest teacher. Anyway, I might regard it as particularly lucky that here within the Swiss region, where there is still relatively speaking the opportunity for peaceful objectivity, that precisely due to this possibility of peaceful objectivity a deeper understanding can enter as well and point out the necessity for the mutual social understanding of humanity indicated in these four lectures, and calling for action. After all, within the pain and suffering which come along during the course of events and in destiny which various members of humanity can experience these days, it can give a certain satisfaction that misfortune actually has taught some people a thing or two. So it could happen — if you allow me to bring this, as it is always meaningful not to remain abstract but be actual when relating to the social question — I have incorporated an appeal in my detailed presentation here in short sentences, a call which is actually dedicated towards processes in the whole world but which has found entry into the hearts of those who have been severely tested in Germany and German-Austria by tragedy and educated by tragedy. I have in this appeal tried to present how the founding of the German Reich took place at a time when the developmental possibilities of a newer humanity in such a reestablishment wanted to, in the most imminent sense, enter into the new social task.

Small things were presented in a comprehensive way; yet just what this empire should have done, to place corresponding content into its frames from the developmental forces of modern humanity and steer towards this Threefoldness, this they could not see. The result has been that the rest of the world turned towards Central Europe. How could the rest of the world understand the entitlement of this particular empire's establishment if this establishment did not create what undoubtedly pointed out its right within the international process of humanity?

Therefore, I have believed that a right program, if I may call it that — but you know from the foregoing: this is no program but the reality — therefore I have believed that formulation may be done in the appeal to humanity for a task which could arise from the Europeans who are confronted with the necessity for renewal. After all one can be satisfied that up to yesterday afternoon this appeal had already been supported by more signatures in Germany than the one-time appeal of the ninety-nine intellectuals with unhappy memories, that over a hundred signatures for this appeal in Germany and up to yesterday over seventy signatures out of German-Austria has been made available for this appeal. I mention this because I want to speak from the basis of reality and as a result draw attention to what I believe is needed in the further process of social development, by it not standing alone when it comes down to making it valid for the mutual relationships of one person to another.

So we must first work on the way to a real social solution. This is the next step. Today humanity stands for once in relation to a large part of the civilized world confronting the necessity to look the social problem in the eye. To do so would mean solving a problem — let me say this to you in conclusion — that it is uncomfortable in the highest levels of thinking. Many people will still admit that for a transformation of the institutions, a transformation of the social structure is necessary. Didn't the entire spirit of the lectures, which I allow myself to present, hasn't the whole spirit been one of pointing out that something else is necessary? If Proletarian Marxist educated leaders repeatedly stress that the words of Marxism are the truth: The philosophers interpreted the world and declared: ‘It comes down to thoughts not only explaining the world but transforming it.’ Thus, it happens in today's critical demands of time that not only a half measure but perhaps not even a quarter is done. What is necessary is that thoughts are not only directed to some or other transformation of institutions, or social structures but that it is necessary for thoughts themselves to change. Only out of reformed thoughts will a healthy social organism be able to develop. Institutions hardly please people; to re-think is even less pleasing — but necessary. Unless a person accepts this, it will not be possible to orientate him- or herself, and then they can't cooperate towards the healing of the social organism.

For a long time, the most important considerations and decisions have knocked at the door of the social question. Now it has entered into the house of humanity. It can't be thrown out again because in a certain sense humanity's evolution comes up against an enchantress. It not only works on humanity's outer structure but makes humanity face the need to either re-think or to add tragedy to the already present tragedies, which multiply.

With this, necessities become clear, what needs to be realised if it will not be too late in the relationship that instincts, as I've mentioned, takes on form in order that the understanding between the various classes would no longer be possible. Only then do we approach a healing of the social organism when renewal, what we are waiting for, when health, for which we hope, are not based on old thinking, but that when we make the bold and powerful decision towards the progress of mankind by orientating our forces towards new thinking; because only out of new thoughts will the possibility of life blossom for new generations. This is how you must think the social question has come about, that it has grown out of the conditions of modern life. It will be false to think one can believe in somehow finding a current solution. Socialism isn't a solution or an attempt at a solution, no, modern life and the life of mankind into the future has brought about the social question. It will always be there. In a living, social organism solutions will always be needed. In this a part, a piece of the life of future humanity will have to exist, that in each generation these questions need to be solved out of new forms; this social question which, once it has come up, admonishes and upsets the entire structure of human thoughts and feelings. If we turn to it with our whole heart, with our entire soul, then it will turn to us, not however for our salvation but for our harm.

THE SOCIAL WILL AS THE BASIS TOWARDS A NEW, SCIENTIFIC PROCEDURE.

1st Public Lecture
added to the 4 lectures on the Social Question

by Rudolf Steiner
given at Zurich, 25 February 1919

wn.rsarchive.org/Lectures/GA328/English/eLib2017/19190225p01.html

The theme for this evening's lecture has been requested as "The social will as a basis towards a new, scientific procedure." I don't know exactly what the motives are for proposing this theme, but when the request came to me I found it extraordinarily lucky because it corresponds in tone to what I consider necessary with regard to the facts which the social movement has brought into the present, and is expressed far more clearly than what formerly had been discussed and negotiated regarding the social question in the course of the last decades.

It is possible to follow the development of the social movement over a long time, up to our present times and to notice how the social impulses in their aims tend more and more to the one or other side, having something sneaking into this social will, into the social mood of recent times which can seem like a wrapping of something from quite another time when superstitions ruled in the Middle ages. These superstitions appear now again when you engage yourself deeply in the second part of Goethe's "Faust" and come to the scene where Goethe allows his Wagner to create the Homunculus, the manikin who would like to be on the way to becoming a human being, developed out of the manikin. According to Goethe it depended on Middle Age superstitions to desire the creation of something out of mere theory, mere outer dry and sober facts assimilated in the human mind into something with being, something thought up which becomes alive. The impossibility of taking abstractions drawn from outer life and forming something alive with them, was Goethe's concern in particular. The Middle Ages don't rule our current thinking as such, but it appears to me as a metamorphosis, one could say, in all the impulses and instincts of many of our contemporaries who want to address the social will and allow some superstitions to dominate. One can observe the development of social life, how it has in the course of history up to the present resulted in thoughts developing out of certain principles, certain foundations which they want to accomplish, or, as you can hear from various opinions, they want it carried out themselves, which means, just as through abstract principles the Homunculus was formed, they can create something called a social organism.

Towards such a social organism there is a striving of, what one could call, the unconscious part of modern humanity. It is only necessary to make the following clear, in order to understand this. The social life of humanity as such is admittedly nothing new; it only appears to be different in more recent times. The social structure of a community is determined, in our more recent times, by the human instincts and human subconscious impulses. The most significant aspect of the rising forces of our more recent times is that humanity can no longer remain stuck on mere instinctive will impulses, that simply out of the nature of development it must prepare the form of the social structure out of a conscious will. If it is to be prepared through a conscious will, then the will needs a basis of thoughts which need to be developed in the right way. These thoughts towards its foundation would not be mere thoughts derived out of abstractions but out of reality; they would be thoughts which familiarise one's own will with the forces in natural events which weave within the world's own powers. To a certain extent one must be allied in one's own will with the creative powers of natural existence.

This is something which wide circles of humanity still need to learn. They must learn to think that they actually can't proceed if they think: 'What must happen in order to withdraw from a social structure formed out of a life many experience as intolerable, is to replace it with a feasible social structure.' — One cannot proceed this way. One can't imagine what social illnesses are, to a certain extent. One can only apply one's best aspirations by finding it out of people themselves, how they live together in the community and bring mutual harmony in their reciprocal relationships to unfold what is necessary in these alternate lives, to establish a social structure.

After long years of studying the social question it has come to me that the basic question, which is considered today as a uniform abstract formulation, should be seen in a threefold way: the first, being like a spiritual question, the second, like a question of law and the third as an economic question. What has arisen out of the modern capitalist economic life has developed from the basis of technology and this has hypnotised people's focus in recent times only on to economic life, and have quite drawn away the awareness of the social question beside the economic question to above all also a spiritual question and a question of rights.

I'm going to allow myself to deal with the spiritual question first, not from the basis as perhaps some of you may believe the consideration of spiritual life involves me in particular, but because I am of the conviction that if the Proletarian thinkers of today become unbiased toward the spiritual aspect, in search of a solution for the social question, it can make a contribution to just those realistically orientated observers of the social question, that the spiritual aspect must take a stand first of all. To do so is to develop insight into the soul of those people touched in their real nature by the modern social movement. You need to try and recognise the will impulses of what actually lives in the socialistic orientated circles. Above all, the origins of these will impulses need to be discovered.

You see, as technology and capitalism moved into our more recent human lives, humanity branched off more and more into the so-called ruling class, away from the development in the most varied areas of Proletarianism. Between the Proletarian forces of will and the non-proletarian life today lies a gap, no one can lie about it, a gap which can hardly be bridged if not at least an attempt is made, not only with antiquated thoughts and old will impulses active in the social movement, but with new thoughts and will impulses.

In the course of time a belief has developed within the Proletariat — and one can as far as relationships go, not at all see this belief as something unfounded — a belief has formed that the socially disadvantaged class can expect nothing from the present ruling class if they build on their goodwill, their ideas and so on. There has, if I may say so, developed a deep mistrust between the individual human classes. This mistrust has come out of the origins, which up to now did not play a role in human consciousness, origins which have always been available in the subconscious. As a result, at the start of our more recent times, the bourgeois working class has met with one final important trust and they, not out of their convictions but by feeling, have been tricked out of this final important trust. You see, we are talking about the Proletarian point of view today. Many, also earlier personalities who believed they could bring the Proletarian will and thinking into an expression, actually knew nothing about the origins of these thoughts and will impulses. What comes as challenges out of life itself, living in the social movement actually stands in a remarkable contrast with the challenges and social impulses which are being considered by the Proletarians themselves. If I want to briefly express what I mean, I must say: the Proletarian, the social culture has thus come about, but within the proletarian feelings, within the social culture and the life, rules the inheritance out of just those viewpoints and concepts of life which came about at decisive moments in their historic development.

This decisive moment in the more recent historic development must surely allow the observer to notice that within this development, the newer scientific way of thinking has grown — I ask you to please take note, I don't say natural science but the newer scientific way of thinking — in such a way out of the old spiritual impulses, but that this scientific way of thinking no longer involves the same spiritual power which the old-world view had. The old-world view sent roots and spread into human impulses as the modern scientific way of thinking. The old-world view was capable of sending impulses into the soul, through the person's sensing and experiencing towards solving a stirring question: 'What am I actually as a person in the world?' — Such a power living in the soul has not come through the modern scientific way of thinking. Obviously through a historic necessity, which is no less of a historical disaster, the old-world view positioned itself at a decisive moment in a hostile opposition towards the newer scientific way of thinking instead of allowing it to flow into a fuller friendship which it should have carried into the spiritual life of the soul. So the following facts came about.

The capitalist machine of economic order tore a number of people out of the context of their lives, out of a context in which they had stood up to then which had quite a different relationship with regards to human feelings for their sense of dignity. There existed a connection between what a person was and what he did. Just think about the relationship which clearly continued in the old crafts up to the

13th Century and still continue in remnants later. Out of this relationship a large number of people were thrown at the machine of the modern economic order. Here was no kind of relationship to elements of production; here was no possibility to establish some or other process between the people and what they were actually doing. This is how it came about that this side of human beings, who didn't invent the modern machine age, could ask: 'What am I worth as a human being? What am I really worth?'

This question is not to be answered out of a context, of life having become overpowered and worthless, but the answer is to be found within those who were not dependent on the outer context of life. Here nothing other rose out of these classes than what the machine age and the economic ordering imposed at the same historic time: the result was the modern scientific way of thinking.

The old classes didn't need to apply this scientific way of thinking to their beliefs and to their concept of life; they only needed to apply it to their theoretical principles. They instilled in life traditional impulses inherited from origins of olden times. The Proletarians were the only ones who were torn out of all they could not identify as their concept of life which was connected to the old outlook on life. They were, through their purely outward existence, predestined to take what was new and allow it to enter their soul content. So this Proletarian is, as paradoxical as it sounds, as unbelievable as many may see it, the actual, purely scientifically orientated person.

To acknowledge the entire scope of this fact one should not only think about what one has learnt about the Proletarian Movement but one needs to be transported through one's destiny by the possibility to think with the Proletarian, with the thoughts of such people who from one or the other side became the carriers of the Proletarian Movement. One could clearly sense what follows, as it spread itself from olden times into the direct social present.

Isn't it true, you could say: 'Yet, the scientific way of thinking still has been extensively accepted in middle-class circles.' — If you consider intelligent middle-class circles, you will think about people whose beliefs are quite scientifically orientated: yet in their feelings, in their entire life experience, they stand within relationships which are not totally determined by scientific orientation. A person can be a materialistic thinker in modern times, can call him or herself cnlightened, call themselves atheists, can acknowledge it as an honest conviction, but can't renounce all the rest of their experiences out of the old connections of life which have not originated from a scientific orientation but which had emerged out of times which carried spiritual impulses — as has been sketched as a force, in the foregoing.

Purely scientific orientation itself works quite differently. I don't say, the scientist, because obviously the scientific orientation influenced quite uneducated Proletarians: but it works quite differently where it has been imposed as a view of life on to the Proletarian.

I want to clarify this by an example. For many years I shared a podium with *Rosa Luxemburg* who has passed away in such a tragic way. She addressed the theme of "Science and the Worker." I need to repeatedly think how she stirred a large audience towards being aware that actually all prejudices which are in relation to human social situations are human classifications according to the old ruling classes and this is connected to representations of what old spiritual viewpoints contained. The modern Proletarian, she believed, originated not solely from angelic, divine origins but they had at one time indecently climbed around trees from animalistic origins which she had developed, on the basis that as she had followed their development, she could substantiate the conviction: a human being is the same as another human being. All previous classification was based on some or other form of prejudice. — You should not consider her formulation but what kind of force such words had on the proletarian natured soul.

Purely considering the concept, I actually meant to say: The Proletarian is completely "scientifically" orientated in his point of view in more recent times. The scientific orientation failed to fill his soul in such a way that it could answer the question: 'What am I actually, as a human being?'

Where did the Proletarian get this point of view? What is the basis of this scientific orientation which he sometimes had to receive in such a false way? It is after all a science. He took it as the inheritance of the middle-class people. It developed out of an old viewpoint of life, from within middle-class people at the transition into the more recent machine and capitalistic age, when machines and capitalism overpowered the people.

The following which is often heard with corresponding colouring is this: within the Proletarians their spiritual life became something which can be experienced as an ideology. This is heard most often when the background of the Proletarian view of the world is dissected: art, religion, science, ethics, law and so on are ideological mirror images of the outer materialistic reality.

However, this experience that everything is like this, that spiritual life is ideological, this didn't originate from within the Proletarians, the Proletarians received it as a dowry from the bourgeoisie. This last and big belief which the Proletarians took in from the middle-class was a result of the nourishment it received, spiritual nourishment for the soul. It could well be that as it was exposed to spiritual life, as it was called out of the old relationship to the machine and introduced into the social structure, that it could only look at what had developed as knowledge about the people and the world; it could only look upon what it had received out of the bourgeoisie: through belief, dogmatically — I could call it — it acquired ideology from the bourgeoisie. It hadn't entered into the convictions but as an experience of disillusionment which it had to be if one does not look at the spiritual as something which is created out of itself, containing a higher reality, but if one looks at it is a mere ideology. Within the subconscious awareness of a large number of carriers of the social movement it wasn't known but was clearly being experienced: 'We have met the bourgeoisie with a strong trust, we have entered into an inheritance which should have brought us the salvation of our souls and the strength to carry it though. The middle classes didn't bring this; only ideology, which has no reality and which contributes nothing towards the support of life.'

One can argue a lot whether ideology is really the basis of spiritual life, or not. It doesn't come down to that but it comes down to spiritual life being experienced by the majority as an ideology, and so the soul becomes desolate, remains empty, the centrifugal spiritual force becomes paralysed and the result is what has happened today: The stripping of the social will from belief that somehow something spiritual could have developed, somewhere rise as a centre, a real centre from which our world view or something similar can bring salvation, also in relation to the desired formation of the social movement. I would like to say: as a negative, spiritual life has been incorporated into the development of the modern Proletarian humanity above all things; as a positive, that it demands yearnings from these people. It demands soul-supporting and as an inheritance has been given the depletion of the soul.

This is something which blows and runs quietly though our entire present day social movement which can't be grasped by concepts, which in fact makes out the form of one of the branches — we got to know three — of the present day social movement. As soon as one perceives that this is so, one can correctly ask: Where has it come from and how can it be remedied? Instead of letting will be paralysed, this social will, how can it be fired up and empowered? This is a question one must ask oneself.

Now an event occurred when the spiritual life came to a decisive point which I've indicated already. The ruling class at the time was through their situation in life connected to, what we today call, the state. It has often been stressed by some individuals — I can't enter into this today due to our limited time in how true this is — it has often been stressed that modern humanity believe that what we call the state, today, has always existed in this way. That is completely untrue. What we call the state, which for example in the Hegelian world appeared as an expression of the divine itself, was basically only a product of thinking in the last four to five Centuries. The social organism of earlier times was quite different.

Just take a single fact, take the most recently appeared fact that the free schools of earlier times, which were independently built opposite the state, were filled out by state institutions, and that, to some extent, the state had become the custodian of mankind's spiritual goods. This happened due to the civil interests in the beginning of more recent times.

The state was there to let the folk grow their souls towards it; they connected all their needs to it. Out of this impulse grew a new relationship between spiritual goods and the state, made the state the custodian of the spiritual goods of mankind and demanded from those approaching the custodian that their lives be actually defined by it.

If one looks deeper into the inner weaving of the human spiritual goods then it involves not only an outer administration of the spiritual goods — the legislation regarding universities as part of the state, of schools, of folk schools becoming part of the state — but that the state is determining the content of the spiritual goods.

Certainly mathematics doesn't have a state characteristic, but other branches of our spiritual goods have their character, have sustained the unification of these spiritual goods with interests of the state in more recent times. This growing together is not without participation of becoming an ideology from the side of spiritual goods. The spiritual goods can only really protect its own true worth, which it carries within, when it can govern itself through its own forces, when out of its direct initiative can give the state what it is, when it however doesn't receive demands from the state.

Certainly there will still be many today who will see no fundamental social facts in what I've just said. They will however see that, in reality, only the ruling spirit of mankind can give laws, when this spirit is separated and stands independently from the outer state organisation. I know that kind of objections can be made against this but this is not important. What is relevant is that the spirit, in order to unfold itself properly, calls for the ability to always develop out of the direct free initiatives of the human individual.

In this way one arrives at the true form of one of the members of the modern social question, that one considers the spiritual life in the right way and see the necessity, that whatever is pushed into the structure of the state is gradually brought out again, so that it can unfold its own supporting power and then work back again, just because when it is freed, while it develops independently with the other members of the social structure, it can as a result really work on the social structure.

If one wants to talk about the practical aspects of the first member of the social question, one must say: The tendency of development for the spiritual life must be denationalized in the widest sense. If the spiritual life member should be denationalised which probably appears today as a paradox, one can speak in this way: the relationship in which a ruling individuality appears to people, who is involved in criminal or private law involving people — one can in certain psychological orientated circles still see that, but taking the thing from quite the wrong side — one so personal, the direction belongs directly to what must be considered internally as spiritual life. So I am counting all which is relevant in religious convictions, all artistic life, all which is related to private and criminal law, to move towards developing the tendency for denationalization.

Why should anyone who hears about mass regulation immediately think about violent revolution? Even in socialist circles of more recent times, people are gradually not thinking like this anymore. I also don't consider that from one day to the next, everything can be denationalized; but I think that through the social will humanity can enter into measures here and there — it must also happen here or there on a daily basis — towards a re-orientation for such a gradual detachment of the spiritual life from that of the state. You can imagine realistically what is actually meant by this.

The state we must see as something which in recent times has grown out of the ruling classes, created out of a particular soul of the middle classes becoming educated. To the state this bourgeoisie has now contributed not only spiritual life, but also what the later human development has overpowered in the social organism: namely the economic life. This economic life having been introduced into the life of the state has introduced the further nationalisation of traffic interests, post, railways and so on. This has resulted in a certain superstition towards the state, towards nationalised orientated associations. The last remainders of these beliefs are the beliefs of the socialist orientated people: that actually the salvation of a communal administration is only possible through a communal economy. Also, that is an inheritance accepted by the middle-class viewpoint and way of thinking.

Now spiritual life has been put on one side and the economy on the other side; in the middle, the state is positioned.

You can ask what will actually remain of the state? As we will soon see in what follows, the economic life couldn't tolerate being mixed into actual state life. Perhaps we can reach a clear picture of this question if we clearly envisage what the bourgeois classes found in the developing modern state. They found the stronghold of their rights in this state.

Let us now examine what the actual laws represent. I'm not thinking about criminal law or about private law as it isn't in the relation of one person to another, because I'm thinking of public law. Public law belongs, for example, to the dealings of ownership. What is property finally? Ownership is only the expression of the authorization of something which one personally and alone may possess and work on. Ownership has sprouted from a law. Everything which we see as material objects has its roots in the relationship of people to laws. Such laws have in our recent times, before the conception of our modern state, rejected the bourgeoisie earlier and everything connected to them; such laws found themselves best protected when they took on everything which referred to such laws as those from within the state itself.

So the tendency started of economic life being ever more drawn into the life of the state. The state penetrates the structure of the economic life with a number of laws. Now, these laws should in no way be taken in their future development to the state life. The social will must gradually develop towards the precise differentiation between everything comprising the life of law, what spiritual life actually is and what the economic life is.

The modern social movement makes it particularly clear that the ruling circles haven't taken anything of the life of rights from their modern state. While much has been taken out of the economic life, also out of the purely isolated economic life, and incorporated into the legal state structure, there is something which has not been incorporated into this legal structure and that is the labour of the Proletarian workers. This labour of the Proletarian workers was left within the circulation of the economic processes.

This struck most deeply into the minds of the modern Proletarians and could be made clear through Marxism and its followers — there is always the labour market just as there is a goods market. Just like goods are offered on the goods market and there is a demand for it, so you bring your labour — the only thing you own — on to the labour market, and it is only valid as goods. You are sold like goods; you stand in the more modern economic process as goods.

Through this we come to the true form of the second modern social claim. This is expressed from out of a certain subconscious sense regarding human worth; the modern Proletarian found it unbearable that his labour was bought and sold as goods on the labour market.

Certainly, the theory of the socialist thinker states: 'It has come about through the objective laws of the economic life itself; the force of labour was placed on the market like other goods.' This is in the awareness, perhaps even in the awareness of the Proletarians. However, in their subconscious, something else was weaving. In their subconscious the continuation of the old slavery prevailed, the old question of serfdom. In the subconscious one only saw how the entire person during the time of slavery could be bought and sold, that later somewhat less of the person was in bondage and all that was now left over was the labour of the workers. With this he allows himself to be taken completely into the economic process. This he felt was impossible, as unworthy.

From this the second social demand has come about in more recent times: disrobing labour from the characteristic of goods.

I know that still today many people think: 'How can that be done? How else is it at all possible to organise economic life than through the remuneration of work activity, labour?' — With this you have already bought it! However, one needs to hold something up against it, which *Plato* and *Aristotle* already took as obvious and said it was evident, that there has to be slaves. So modern thinking needs to be forgiven if it finds it necessary to carry labour to the market.

Now one can't always imagine what will perhaps be a reality in the near future. Today however we must ask: How can labour be disrobed from the character of goods? It can only happen if it is drawn up in the area of a pure legal state, such a state which eliminates it from the spiritual life on the one side, as characterized earlier, and eliminated on the other side from all that belongs to, what was characterised earlier, as the economic process. If we divide the entire social organism, or we think of it as divided into three members: into an independent spiritual life, into legal life and economic life, then we have instead of Homunculus in the area of economy a real Homo in the area of the economic life, then we have our spiritual eyes focused on the real social organism which is alive, not one made up of chemical agents.

I don't really want to enter into a game of analogy between biology and sociology — that's far from me — neither fall into the mistake of *Schäffle* nor *Meray* in his "World Mutation"; I don't want to go into all of that, it is not relevant here. What is of relevance is to see how, in a single natural human organism, three independent systems rule — I have presented this scientifically, at least as a sketch, in my last book "**Riddles of the Soul**" — likewise in the social organism three independently applicable systems need to be seen: the spiritual system, the judicial system — now the system of public rights, as mentioned where private and criminal law are excluded — and the actual economic system.

However, if you have between the spiritual and the economic life, the regulated state life, the regulated judicial life, then you have something which is capable of life inserted into the social organism, just as in the natural human organism you find the relatively independent systems of circulation, lung-heart system and circulation system, the heart-lung system between the head system and digestive system. Then again if it is fully developed from its own basis as merely economic — we think of a democratic administration on the basis of judicial life — if each one can equally have a say about his rights, that the only basis of ruling will be according to the relationship of one person to another, then the incorporation of labour in the economic process will be something quite different than the case is now.

You see, I'm not giving you some or other principle, or theory: this is how it must be done when the power of labour is to be disrobed from its characterisation of goods — but rather, I say to you: 'We must place people in such a division in the social members that, through their actions, through their thoughts, through their will, a viable social organism is created.' — I don't want to offer general remedies but I only want to say how humanity must become members of the social organism in order for their healthy social will to continuously result in making the social organism capable of life. In this way I will, in place of theoretical thinking, introduce intimately related and trustworthy thoughts. What will happen if, despite economic life, there would exist a foundation which maintains and governs itself out of its own forces, and out of this purely human foundation, employment laws can be negotiated? Then something will come about which work in a similar way into the economic process as does the natural foundation of economic processes. We very clearly see these natural foundations of the economic process when we really study the economic process. They regulate the economic process in such a way that its regulation deprives a person of what he or she can do themselves, in the economic process. Isn't it so, you only have to observe the obvious?

Just take for once — I want to use radically clear examples — the fact that in certain regions, rather removed from our area, the banana is an extraordinarily important item. However, the work which involves bringing bananas to a place where they can be consumed is exceptionally little from our point of view, in comparison with products in our natural European region; bringing wheat from its point of origin right through to its point of consumption. This work which renders the bananas consumable is nothing in comparison to wheat, roughly compares it is as one to one hundred, or the relationship could be even greater than one to a hundred. So, one hundred times more effort is needed than that of bananas, to bring wheat to the point of consumption. So we can quote the biggest variables within the economic area which exist in connection with the regulation of economic life. These are not only dependent on what a person contributes: it depends on the yield of the earth, other relationships and so on; these things place themselves within the economic life as a constant factor, like people are one of the independent economic factors. This is how it can be seen from the one side.

Now consider for yourself the labour laws as quite separate on the other side from the economy, then it will, when it no longer has economic interests in the determination of working hours, in the application of labour independently contributing to an independent purely person to person interrelationship, it will create something independent of the economic life, which plays from the other side into this economic life, just like each side plays from the natural foundations of given factors.

One must orientate the formation of prices, which has actual worth in the goods market to how the natural factors work. One will in future, when the social organism should be viable, also have to address how production should take place, how the circulation of goods should take its course. When this commodity circulation does not determine remuneration, working hours and labour law, but when it is independent of commodity circulation, of the goods market, in the region of the state life, purely out of human endeavours, purely out of mere human points of view agree about the working hours, then it will be so that one commodity will cost as much as it will cost for the time needed to produce that particular work, which is however regulated through independent economic life, because economic life today for instance regulates employment so that the price of goods often has to regulate the economic process in working hours and employee-employer relationships. The opposite will appear by correctly dividing the members of the social organism.

These relationships can only be indicated today. You can see, however, that they come out of a social intention which is quite different from what has placed us into such a sad situation within world events; they come out of a social will which has not originated from some non-profitable spinning of human thoughts, spinning as one has to so that this or that is done in the right way, but they come out of thoughts which are so familiar with reality that it doesn't come to light when people in this or that relationship in this or that way become members of the social organism. Then they will, because they have become members of the social organism in a healthy way, be able to determine laws, then they will work in the right way.

One only has to have experienced how other social intentions determined relationships in real life, even in the then already conquered Austria. It was a state, but a state does not live purely as a life of laws; in a state, there lives, in quite a pronounced way, the economic life which has sprung from the interests of single human circles. Just think how the old Austrian parliament was up to the end of the nineties (1890's). Out of this parliament's representation originated relationships which played right into the catastrophe of war. This parliament consisted of the four curiae: the Chamber of Commerce, the great land owner, from the curia of the cities, markets and industrial sites and the curia of the established economic circles. These economic circles were not represented on the basis of an economic parliament but their interests determined the being of the state, therefore public laws were determined according to them. Just as it is impossible for a confessional inclined party, which the last German Reichstag was, to be created and influence institutions of the legal life of the state out of definitions, just so little is a social organism viable which is destined to determine the economic circles of the legal life. The life of rights must develop separated from that; only out of the relationship of one person to another, considered in a completely democratic manner. Then the rights life will regulate in a corresponding manner the threefold organism, with on the one side the economic life and on the other side the natural foundation of this economic life.

Within the economic life, which in turn has established representatives from the most varied fields, pure economic factors and interests would be needed. One would then have a social organism — if I might express myself according to the habits of the time — with three classes, three areas, each creating its own laws and own management. They will stand in a relationship, one could call it, as sovereign states and if they continue, they reckon with one another. That could invite complications, make the people uncomfortable; but it is the one and only way to make a healthy social organism viable in future. The economic life itself can only be determined out of its factors when only economically active interests appear from its foundation, which can only be determined through the necessary relationships between production and consumption. These relationships between production and consumption can only result in the economy from the associative basis, an associative basis as it could have been in the trade union, cooperative context. However today the trade union, cooperative context still maintains the character out of the state from which it has grown. They need to grow into the economic life, must become mere serving bodies of the economic life. Only then will the social organism develop in a healthy way.

I know that what I've been saying will appear extraordinarily radical. Whether it appears radical or not, is not important. What is important is for the social organism to be workable, that people, in their starting from the old instinctive social life moving towards the conscious social life, are permeated with impulses which come out of insight of how one needs to stand within the totality of the social organism. People today are considered uneducated if they don't know their multiplication tables; a person is considered uneducated if he does not know something he is supposed to know as education, but a person is not considered uneducated if he has no social awareness, or if his soul is within the social organism in a state of sleep. This is something which has to change fundamentally in future! It would be different if a judgement would consider that, what belongs to the most elementary schooling should include being equipped with a social will, just as much as one should be equipped with the multiplication tables. Today every person should know what three times three is. In the future, it would not appear more difficult to know the relationship between capitalism and ground rental if I want to choose something out of today's life. It should not be more difficult in future than to know that three times three is nine. However, this knowledge will become the foundation for a healthy involvement in the social organism which means a healthy social life. A healthy social life needs to be strived for.

In a healthy human consciousness, it is preparing itself, as I have said. One only has to have an inkling for what is being prepared and what strives towards revelation and form in our more recent time.

Just think back to the great ideals of the French Revolution: Freedom, Equality and Brotherhood. Whoever followed these ideas in the minds of people who have in the course of time experienced it as a destiny, knows, how often they have struggled with the logic within the contradiction which exist in Freedom on the one side, which point to personal initiatives, and Equality on the other side, which should be brought about in the centralization of the state orientated social organism. This is not possible. Yet, the solution for this confounding has emerged in our more recent time. Why capitalism today has not yet understood the concept of a threefold social organism is due to the concept of a completely centralised state.

If you grasp the idea which already today appear in this intention which is expressed in the ideals of Freedom, Equality and Brotherhood, then it is easy to understand that it is being considered from the point of view of the threefold organised social organism. Its first member would be the spiritual life. It should be completely permeated with the idea, the principle, of freedom. Here everything should be based on the free initiatives of people and it can be so, would be most fruitful, if it is stated this way. With reference to the constitutional state, in relation to what is between the spiritual and the economic life regulated by the being of the state, the actual political system exists, which has to permeate everything regarding the equality of relationships between people. With reference to the economic life, the one and only thing which is valid is Brotherhood, social community living the outer and inner life of one person through the other.

In the economic life within the social organism, interest is the ruling factor. This interest however brings quite a specific characteristic into the economic member. Why is it apparent that basically everything comes out of economic life? It all comes down to economic life, that in the best, most appropriate manner, the economic life shows it can also be consumed. I'm talking about consumption in the narrower sense where the spiritual is excluded. Consumption can refer for instance to labour, human labour. This is felt by the modern person: becoming a mere element of consumption in terms of his labour. He even has to, like he earns interest through his labour, through spiritual production, also inherit interests through his rest, through his calm capacity for the spiritual. The human being becomes consumed in the economic life. He has to pull himself continuously out of the economic life by the other two members of the healthy social organism, if he doesn't want to be completely consumed within the economic life.

The social question is not the same in modern life as when it originated and perhaps could be solved, and was actually solved. No, the social question exists as something which has entered modern life and can no longer be avoided in the future of humanity. There will always be a social question in the future. However, this social question will not for once, not through this or that measure, be solved, but could be regulated, through the continuous intentions of people which means that those who use people in the economic process, should be regulated from the political standpoint and forever balance out the consumption with spiritual production, through the independent spiritual organism.

Whoever has seen over the last decades how the social question has developed — and it has relatively not been all that long ago that the social question has taken on its present form — whoever has observed in intimate detail how the social question has developed out of its origins, could in relation to the social intentions/will and its focus for the future form of human life, arrive at thoughts which could be characterised in the following way.

Many people, even enlightened people, don't see the social question as something existentialistic. In my youth, I became acquainted with an Austrian minister who officiated over the Bohemian-German border and made the most grotesque declaration: "The social question stops at Bodenbach." I remember very clearly how a large group of the first social democratic miners marched past my parents' house, heading for their gathering. I noticed how the social will had come about, not as thoughts about a social movement but through the communal life of the social movement. I had to say to myself, much has to be done and many mistakes have to be made! Even with socialistically orientated thoughts of more recent times, these mistakes were quite numerous. It appears that exactly in this area people's minds developed in such a way that they didn't experience this. The mistakes became terribly widespread.

Out of such a spirit of obscrvation I have endeavoured to speak to you tonight about the social will. You have invited me as member of a community who studies what the social intention of humanity's healing should bring in future.

Those older people, like me for example, who speak to people who through the decades can look back, know about all that had to be gone through to get to the present moment. Then again you find some things that need to be gone through, in addition also the conviction that the mistake was not fruitless, that even today when the facts are expressed often in a frightening way, people manage to be strong enough to find the way out of what the biggest part of today's humanity has experienced as unbearable.

It is in this sense that I ask you to accept what I have allowed myself to speak about this evening. The facts speak clearly in some areas. The facts also clearly say: the more people, who are still young, can now take up a true, viable social intention, the more will the human social organism be viable and efficient. Whoever wishes to speak the word, let him do so. Doctor Boos, who has given a lecture about a week ago, announced that he was willing to have discussions.

A speaker says something (stenographic details incomplete).

Dr Steiner: What you have claimed has taken on a form as a result of you not considering what must come to the fore through the relatively independent formation, on the one hand of the constitutional state and on the other, the economic life. The labour organisations which are partly production companies or consumer companies, or even could have connections between both, are only involved with economic factors which take place within the economic life itself.

The regulation of labour law is preferred by a relatively independent state. Here nothing is decided other than on a democratic basis, I call it, as relevant to the relationship of one person to another. This is why I mention this regarding the basis of the purely democratic state, that a link exists between both factors, on this basis people stand equally before the law. As a result, the mere wishes of single economic organisations will come to an end because they must balance out the democratic legal life with the interests of other circles.

So, this is just what should be processed, a remedy should be considered towards anything damaging, which would certainly develop if for instance the working hours are fixed within the organisation of the economic life. Economic organisations should only be involved with the economy itself: in other words, the regulation in the sense of labour laws. By contrast, the fixing of working hours, only underlying the state corporation, involves the relation of one person to another.

We must not forget what a great change can develop between one person and another with one-sided interests grinding it down. Self-evidently, nothing can be totally perfect in the world, but one-sided interests will be grinded down in the democratic state structure which has its basis of equality between people.

Just consider for instance what happens when a certain economic organisation is interested in a project of short duration — they will have to be comfortable with balancing this with the interests of the individuals who would suffer during this short working time. If one doesn't consider some or other subconscious force then it would — just like in a natural organism it would always in an approximately natural way result in how many men and how many women there are, which obviously is no strict natural law nor will it become one — it would also prevent something unhealthy being created when in the right way the single factors of the social organism cooperate and not develop individual small interests, which are most harmful to others.

The foundation of my way of thinking differs from many other social thinking patterns due to the latter being more abstract. Logically the one can easily be derived from the other; results flow from one logic into another. Crucial to such questions is only actual life experience. Obviously I can't prove logically — no one can — that a discrepancy of interests may enter into such a future organism, but accept that when the forces within their own circles, which are appropriate to them, can develop, then it will be a humane development. I mean, if you consider what I have wanted to present, the fixing of working time out of the purely economic process in the legal circle of the state, then this damage will be able to develop in practical areas. This is what I wanted to add.

Another speaker says something (stenographic details incomplete).

Dr Steiner: I would like to comment on the honourable previous speaker's words as follows. Understandably with every lecture it is not possible to say everything one wants to in a single lecture, and I don't know which omissions our previous honourable speaker's conclusion has been drawn from in my lecture where I gave no opinion regarding the modern worker psyche, that I don't want to take the modern labour movement into account, and so on. Every person does it in his own way. I have for many years, for example, been a teacher in the various fields of a workers' educational school and have given rise to speech exercises in political organisations. I am entitled to be aware of a large number of workers who present their speeches today, speeches they have learnt to give as a result of my speech exercises. During these speech exercises all possible kinds of questions were discussed, questions which actually were not far from the most intimate particulars of the workers' psyche. So I don't know — I had naturally no reason to place this particular practical side of my social activities and intentions out in the open, but I can't quite rightly understand out of which omissions my talk should come from what went before, that I should be so far removed from the practical labour movement.

Certainly it is obvious that within the modern social movement the worker himself should be considered. Just contemplate by yourselves, what I have been stressing the entire evening regarding how things can actually appear within the Proletarians. I have spoken about the Proletariat as such; you would have noticed if you were listening attentively, how my belief has woven my lecture into a practical presentation as to what lives in a practical way in the proletarian labour force of today.

Regarding the accusation that I have perhaps been too one-sided in my presentation of what seems to me the fundamental meaningful fact, that the middle-class thinking methods will be conquered by the labour force, particularly by the leaders of the working class, this declaration which I have done and which I have drawn from single instances has made it clear from one side, really more accurate through the study of the workers' psyche and the entire modern labour movement.

I would like to add an example which I would like to draw your attention to. A Russian author who I know personally has recently pointed out to me in an unusual way how a philosophy adhered to by younger people in Zurich has played a big role: the *Avenarius* philosophy which for their part has certainly grown out of the middle-class substrate. I can hardly imagine that Avenarius considered how his philosophy would play such a role in the Russian labour movement as it is playing today. As far as I know it is strongly represented, right in Zurich, by *Adler* who translated the natural scientific derived philosophical conviction of *Mach*. Both these philosophic directions are to some extent the official philosophies of

Bolshevism, of the most radical socialism. The Russian author *Berdjajev* said in a lecture — it is contained in the translation of a very interesting book about "Russia's political soul" — in this lecture Berdjajev has in a very clear manner worked out the political soul.

So you can give a multitude of examples; I could give you numerous examples which are similar to those which I took from the address of the deceased *Rosa Luxemburg*, which would prove to you that the last important heirloom, deeply interwoven with the workers movement and the middle-class life, is the scientifically orientated method of thinking. The possibility to make spiritual life into an ideology is of middle-class origin. The middle-class, if such a categorization may be made, firstly took scientifically orientated methods of thinking in the region of natural knowledge, and made it into an ideology. They did not transfer it within their class over on to scientifically orientated thinking. This latter consequence only then attracted the proletarian thinking. Certainly, proletarian thinking also drew other consequences but these consequences were drawn out of the basis which today is clearly recognisable as rooted within the middle-class' scientific method of imagination, which now created something further. The importance of this should not be misunderstood.

That which dwelled within the totality, which has developed a deep interest for the participation of the modern worker psyche in the modern labour movement, waited, I want to say, with a certain concern on the one side, but also with a certain inner satisfaction on the other side for the moment when it would appear within the modern socialist movement. What now lies in the subconscious will one day be noticed, brought into awareness and it will be said: 'Aha, this we had in our soul's higher thinking' — if I might use this expression — 'in our soul's higher thinking, and it must come to the fore. We have the desire for our human dignity to be scientifically orientated; this is what the middle-class line of inheritance of science has now made possible. We must look for a spiritual life elsewhere.'

I believe in any case that when this moment arrives, when the entire, full longing surfaces out of a specific side of modern people only, namely the proletarian people — if it has not come into full expression in modern times — when this longing in the modern Proletariat has reached its complete education of the scientific way of thinking in their world view, with the power of old religions, when this has happened that it no longer depends on them being goods, drawn as the consequence out of the middle-class thinking methods, then one will be able to argue that the fruitful organization of social will has arrived.

To mere socialism and in its relation to what the previous honourable speaker offered, regarding the philosophy of *Bergson*, I believe one should not make such dogmatic statements. Understandably I don't want to discuss such philosophic questions today. The previous speaker said that Bergson was a typical representative of the bourgeois thinking methods. If this is so then socialism would have developed out of Bergson's philosophy, derived directly out of bourgeois foundations! Today one can for instance refer to Bergson's philosophy as containing many "Schopenhauer-isms" and that Bergson was much more influenced by Schopenhauer than any of you can imagine.

Now, should one want to discuss such a thing in detail, then one has to be able to argue extensively. I can't do this today but I only mention this to you because there are within the proletarian world sensitive thinkers, for instance, *Mehring*, Franz Mehring, who is really in many ways similar to Bergson; he characterised Schopenhauer as the representative of the most bourgeois philistinism in philosophy!

One can have different views about these things and I don't believe one should be dogmatic about it. One can have the view that Bergson is an advanced philosopher who has irrational elements within his philosophy. However, one could ask what an irrational element has to do with the social question. A Proletarian can be just as irrational as a middle-class person. I don't quite understand what this whole irrational element has to do with it. Here one already has to draw a dogmatic precondition: Bergson is the absolute example of a modern philosopher; if the Proletarians really want to think, they must become Bergsonians, not so? This involves the whole issue.

Undoubtedly there are tendencies which appear in the most varied areas of life, tendencies which focus themselves in the direction I have characterised. It would really be sad to order human life, if it is always going so straight, to go over, I would say, and always evolve it in the opposite direction from the straight one! Not so, this can't of course be the case. I would even say in the area of the judiciary, certain things are fuelled by quite psychologically orientated people. Such innumerable examples can of course be cited but it is also a secondary derivation if one doesn't really validate it but merely offers a favourite opinion. Certainly one may sympathise with things which have been said about impulses that have principles according to historic periods; but without going into the latter further — if one wants to go into all these things I will have to keep you here for a very long time — so without further examination into references I want to say the following: very many people are inwardly obstinate when one mentions threefoldness, which I spoke about today. They say three different branches which are directed and guided by different principles are not possible.

However, I haven't spoken about three different members which are directed by three different principles, but about a threefold social organism! Just consider that this threefold social organism in our time must gradually find its whole way of thinking in a corresponding way, like for instance the ancient subdivisions which you find with Plato and which were then justified. Someone once said to me after my lecture:

"So we have once again a reference to Plato: the nutritionists/guardians, the fighters/auxiliaries and the producers/labourers/educational state." Actually, what I have said is the opposite of divisions into nutrition, defence and educational states because people are not divided into classes but divisions are sought for in the social organism. We human beings will simply not be divided up! It can well be that the same person who is active in the spiritual member, is active in the judicial and even the economic member. The human being is as a result emancipated from such one-sidedness in some or other member of the social organism. It is therefore not important that people should be divided into such independent classes when a healthy social organism is developed, but that the social organism orders itself according to its own laws. That is the radical difference. Earlier, people were divided. Now, according to the way of thinking relevant to our time, the social organism will be divided by itself so that people can look at their life situation according to their needs, their relationships and abilities and how to be active in one or the other division. For instance, it will be quite possible that in future an economically active person may at the same time be a deputy in the field of the purely political state. He will then obviously make his economic interests effective in a different way as he would in relation to the field of the constitutional state. The three divisions provide the demarcation of their territories. Everything doesn't get confused and allow them to get mixed up.

It is better if the things are separated. There are of course the same human systems which are differentiated into the one or the other branch. Just as in the natural human organisation — above all I don't want to play the game of analogy but still need to mention this — there are three centralized parts: the nerve-sense system, lung-breathing system and the digestive system, there are three members in the social organism. This is something which doesn't yet belong to ordinary thinking habits, which I believe however, will be able to find its way into thinking habits and that people would not take it less thoroughly, I think, than when they only grapple with their own favourite opinion.

Dr Roman Boos: May I be permitted to refer to a question addressed to the speaker in relation to the field of criminal law? Now, when there was talk about the freedom of judges, was there also a breach against the statement that no punishment without law will be made — it seems to me this is what is meant, that criminal law as such should not be given out of free spiritual life but out of the political member, that the question possibly contains a misunderstanding with Dr Weiî[2] who stated that an offence is made against the principle that no punishment could be given if no specific law has not been broken. May I ask you to say more about this?

Dr Steiner: Isn't it true that in this question you obviously touch on the system of public law with the system of practical jurisdiction? What I stressed is the separating of practical judging. For this reason, I used the expression "judging," expressly the practical judging from the general public legal life, which I thought should be central in healthy social organisms whose public political life should see to it, that a specific law will determine a procedure. That judging can't be done in the most arbitrary way is quite self-evident. However, I haven't considered such things which are abstract and in their abstraction, they are more or less obvious. Today I have also not spoken about the scope of the law but about the social organism and about the social will. Now I ask you with reference to this theme, to consider the following.

You see, I have nearly spent as much of my life in Austria as in Germany. I could get thoroughly acquainted with the Austrian life; you may believe me that it is not an impulsive assertion if I say that much of what has taken place in the so-called state recently is connected to events which during the (eighteen) seventies and eighties had resulted from deep incongruities. Don't forget that in such a state as Austria, in other fields it isn't as radically characterised, but is present in some or other form as well — particularly because in Austria the various language regions are mixed and overlap and you can for instance have the experience that a German, when he is by chance involved in some or other circuit court officiated by a Czech judge who can't speak German, is convicted by a Czech in a language he fails to understand. He doesn't know what he is convicted of and what has happened to him; all he notices is that he is led away. Just so is the reverse case when a German judge who can't speak Czech, judges a Czech who can't understand German. What I am indicating is the individual arrangement, the free formation of relationships of the judgement to the judge.

So, a state like Austria could expect great success from this. Thus, this impulse resulted in always, over the next maybe five or ten years — relationships shifted continuously — for the convicted being able to choose their judges freely.

(Gap in stenographic record)

This is not simply an object of the spiritual life, but it is foremost an object in the life of the judicial state; in that only one law is focused on, which had originated from a deed and secondly became a law of the state, already concerned with its competence; in each case it will obviously show the concerned result.

However, another question is this: when you look at things more closely you will see that all the solutions to these cases are very consequential. Today I could only give you the initial conditions; I need not talk the entire night but need to continue tomorrow again.

WHAT SIGNIFICANCE DOES WORK HAVE FOR THE MODERN PROLETARIAN?

2nd Public Lecture
added to the 4 lectures on the Social Question

by Rudolf Steiner
given at Zurich, 8 March 1919

wn.rsarchive.org/Lectures/GA328/English/eLib2017/19190308p01.html

When the theme for today's lecture was announced, the question could have been asked: 'From which angle is this going to be approached?' — From some or other research, it could be concluded that now again an understanding needs to be addressed, an understanding so strongly yearned for which has for a long time been imposed as today's capitalistic sea of confusion, and those in it notice that the water is up to their mouths and they are no longer able to swim in this sea. They search for a rescue boat; they would not be able to find such a rescue boat with conditions they usually insist upon. About such an interpretation I don't want to speak this evening. It appears to me that in the time in which we are living, quite other things are necessary. If we look at one another, at what has actually happened and what is going on at present, for those who are searching for such an understanding, it is so terrible.

What is called the 'social question' today has in no way only come about yesterday. In the way one speaks about it today, it is more than half a century old. However, what has actually led up to the social question is much, much older; it has come out of the entire development of modern times and out of the last centuries. When we observe where this development of the last centuries has led up to, then we can sum it up in the following way.

There were a number of people who we can best describe by saying they lived in a capitalistic economic order and felt comfortable living in this capitalist economic order. One hears often enough from these people how far civilization has progressed. One can hear how it has come about that humanity has reached such a stage in which not only distant single countries and continents but over world oceans they could quickly come to an understanding; how far humanity has come through a certain education and taken part in what they called spiritual life, imagining they had reached impressive heights in our time.

I don't need to mention all the praise declarations about this direction in our modern civilization. However, modern civilization has developed out of a foundation. Without this foundation, it is inconceivable; it thrives from this foundation. What was in this foundation? In this foundation there were increasingly more people who out of their deepest soul sensitivities had to let the call be heard: 'Does modern life give us what our human existence is worth? Why have we been condemned by modern civilisation?' — So, modern humanity is ever more split into two divisions: in one in which they feel comfortable or at least feel satisfied in modern civilisation, but out of which they can only feel satisfied because of this foundation, while the other one must create the foundation as their labour, towards a social order in which they can basically have no share.

In the entire process, admittedly something else also developed. It developed in such a way that the carriers of the so-called civilization in the old patriarch conditions could not progress with its numerous illiterates. It meant that of the capitalistic supporters at least a part of the Proletarians, the part in their employ, had to be educated. As a result of this education, the Proletarians developed something which has come to such a frightening expression for those who understand the all too necessary facts. This development brought about the possibility to a large number of people, who had just created the foundation for this modern civilization, to be able to consider their situation; they didn't arrive at an instinctive insight any more but it enabled them to pose this question in the most intensive way: 'Can we have a dignified human existence? How can we acquire a dignified human existence?'

Those who up to now had been the leaders of humanity have in the course of modern economic life brought the economic life as far as they could, into a connection with the modern state. The modern Proletariat could to a certain extent not be excluded from the modern state through the influences of recent times. So it came about that the Proletariat on the one hand within the economic life strived for a dignified existence and on the other hand with the help of the state, tried to win the right.

One can't deny this — the facts teach us — in both directions little has been accomplished. In the manner of the trade unions the modern working community within the economic circulation has tried to accomplish something: there were scraps of what human dignity within a healthy economic order should be. This has been achieved in a way, by state life. On the other hand, the economic and political power of the hitherto leading class of mankind was opposed. So one can say that despite various things having been accomplished in both these directions, today the modern Proletariat is not less challenged by the question: 'What significance is there actually in my work in relation to what each person in the world must consider regarding dignity?'

In contrast to that, for long decades the Proletariat have, in the most varied forms, addressed the leading circles with the cry: 'It can't go on like this!' — On the other hand, hardly an understandable word can be heard in response. The words which do become audible stand in an extraordinary relationship to what the minds of the time should have striven for. Don't we hear it from all possible sides — from the Christian-social side, from the bourgeois-socialist aspirants — some or other statement is being made which could help remedy the dangers which one is believed to be able to see? Was it more basically as ingratiating phrases which came out of various moral, religious deliverances, emerging from those, up to then, leading classes?

These leading circles didn't experience it but the other side of humanity did. The one who feels it from quite another angle than as from empty phrases, the one who experiences it out of the awareness of his or her class, brought into a particular social situation, should form the base for this modern civilisation. And so, some things were done through the trade union, cooperative and also political life, yet something else came about which was more important than the modern Proletarian's work, something which was full of seeds for the future and the facts of the present carried it into abundance. This was created in the following way.

While the ruling classes were amassing their luxuries, which could only be fed and empowered by capitalism, the Proletarian, in the time left over for him, in his meetings sought in the truest sense of the word an education towards a spiritual life. This was something which the earlier ruling classes didn't want to see, that among thousands, yes thousands of Proletarian souls a new culture, a new viewpoint was developing in the people.

Based on the nature of these things, the Proletarian development next proceeded to the viewpoint of considering economic life, because the modern life of the Proletarian was forged by the machine. Into the factory he was packed, harnessed in by capitalism. Here he found his concepts. However, these concepts — I only want to point out how intensely everything connected to Marxism penetrated with meaning into the Proletarian soul — this development was such that very little, really very little reaction was elicited from the leading, up to then ruling classes.

Isn't it typical that those who know about these things must say today: Among the ruling proletarian personalities, among those who really understand the Proletariat, not merely think about the Proletariat but among those individualities who have taken up what could really be considered a fruitful development offered by economic life, among them really live the basic, thorough knowledge of life into which the social organism plays even as the most elite of educators, even the most thoughtful professors of sociology, university professors. It is typical that this circle, whose calling it was so to speak, to concern itself with sociology, with national economics, that it resisted everything which presented itself as an understanding for the modern Proletariat, for as long as possible. Only when the facts threatened and no longer allowed anything else to be permitted, did they accommodate the bourgeois leaders, allowing many Marxist or similar terms to be taken into their national economic system.

That the work of the modern Proletariat was achieved, I would like to call it, achieved in total secrecy towards the leading ruling circles, this I report out of no grey theory; I maintain this because I could observe how this work was being executed. For years I was a teacher in the worker's education school in Berlin, where *Wilhelm Liebknecht*, the dear old servant, could be validated. Partly in this school, partly in what was happening, one had a good extract of every process in action, directed towards a new era developed out of the proletarian consciousness. This should have been considered long ago, but superficially regarded the modern proletarian movement only in terms of wages and daily bread and failed to understand its needs to be considered as a question of human dignity of all people.

On the other hand, it is not really important when people point to the frightening and sometimes cruel events out of the world of facts as originating from the social chaos. Those who understand these things correctly, how they have developed, don't question the connection between these cruelties or terrors to the modern proletarian movement but they clearly take it that the leading classes are at cause for what has come about today.

The world-historical moment only started when the Proletariat began taking responsibility for world historical events. Capitalism, the capitalistic world order particularly in the most recent times worked right into the terrible and in many respects insane catastrophe of the world war.

What can we now see as a central focus in the Proletarian movement and the Proletarian yearnings, which can be considered as the Proletarian progress? In the centre of this we see what the Proletarian experiences regarding that which basically is the cause and which can only be given from the modern economic order to the social organism, because the leading cultural circles are basically only interested in one thing which the Proletarian can give, and that one thing is Proletarian labour. One needs to realize how incisive *Karl Marx's* ideas were, which crossed the tracks of the modern Proletariat in such a way that they had the experience: Above all things clarity must be created in relation to the manner and way in which human labour may flow into the social organism.

Now, it has often been said and illuminated in the widest circles: through the modern economic order, labour has become goods among other commodities. It is typical of the economic life that it exists in the production, circulation and consumption of goods. However, it has happened that the labour of the modern Proletarian has been made into goods.

From this angle, basically everything can be said about the Proletarians. However, the question is usually drawn to one side so that it doesn't appear in the full light but through which one actually gains insights into the statement of the human labour in the healthy social organism. Here the question must be raised which in any case rises out of the Marxist question but it is raised in an even more precise, an even more intense manner. It must be asked: Can human labour ever really be considered as goods?

Through this the question leads to quite a different track. One will in fact ask: How can human labour legitimately be rewarded? How can human labour in any way come to its rights? One can add further: it must be in such a way that human labour earns its pay.

A wage is in some ways nothing other than purchase money for the goods called 'labour power.' However, the power of labour may never be goods! Where the power of labour in the economic process is made into goods, there is a falsehood in the economic process, because in reality something is added which could never be a true component of this reality. On this basis labour can be no goods because it can't have the character which goods is necessitated to have. In the economic process, each item of goods must have the possibility through its value, to be compared with other commodities. Comparability is the basic condition for the 'being-of-goods' (Ware-Sein) of something. The value of human labour can never be compared with the value of some or other commodities or products.

It would have been terribly easy if people had not forgotten how to simply think. Just think about it, for my sake, when ten people in a family work together, each one doing his or her work, how one can take a single contribution out of ten and compare it with the achievement which the ten has produced together? People just don't have the ability to compare the output of goods to the power of labour. Labour stands on quite another basis of social judgement than goods. This is what has perhaps in recent times not been clearly spoken about, but which lives in the experiences of the modern Proletariat.

What lives in the requirements of the modern Proletariat? What lives here in the feelings of the Proletarian is factual criticism, the world historic criticism which simply lies in the life of the modern Proletarians and, hurled into it, everything which the leading circles as a social order have promoted. The modern Proletariat is nothing other than a world historic criticism. Just the knowledge that labour can never be goods, owes its sensation, the basic experience of its existence, which is lived through in recent times as an enormous, an all-encompassing white lie, because labour is sold and according to their being this can never be sold.

That a remedy must be found, as everyone with insight must find obvious, of this the modern Proletariat is convinced. Yet he has been driven into something which not he, but the earlier ruling classes has made of the social organism. He has been pushed out of everything left over and is only drawn into the economic process. Does this not make it clear that he would want to bring about through this mere healing of this economic process and the circulation of the economic life itself, the entire social organism as well? Out of this the ideals have originated in the same way as the ideals the modern Proletariats have lived up to now.

It has been said that because private capitalism has made modern production into a goods production through private means of production, it has resulted in the modern Proletariat coming into the position which only he can experience. The only help can be offered by reverting back to the ancient idea of the cooperative, a cooperative which means that one's production goes over to the other and work towards self-production in which he can't misuse the other on the grounds that he would then be prejudicing himself. The following can also be asked: How would this great cooperative be set up? Here one must take refuge in the framework which has been created in recent times — that of the modern state. The modern state itself must make itself into a big cooperative through which the production of goods gradually is directed to the production of the self-employed.

Here we find the very point which needs to be grasped. One can now say that healing can be found in the modern Proletarians' spiritual life on the one hand, and at the same time discover that where there is a possibility for development in the modern Proletarian's spiritual life, there is a possibility from this step, to take yet another step towards progress.

People who do not agree with this should really not be resented if they are being sincere with honest feelings which they cherish, for they do not yet see results coming from the present Proletarian world view, but it is necessary to point out that this Proletarian world view have seeds of progress, and that this progress should really be striven for — and it can be striven for.

There are those who would admit they became enlightened by what I have already said — about eighteen years ago — in the Berlin trade union house, as a characteristic, and then often again had to emphasise it as a peculiarity of the modern labour movement, which I still maintain as absolute truth. At that time I said: For those who glance over the historic life of humanity with an inner understanding for what has emerged, for them it will be noticeable that this modern Proletarian Movement appears different to all other movements of humanity, basically because — and you might find this grotesque, a paradox even — it stands on a scientifically orientated foundation.

Profound, very profound it was then in this direction as a fundamental, basic requirement of the modern labour movement that the almost forgotten (Ferdinand) *Lassalle's* famous lecture was given entitled “Science and the Worker.” Things need to be looked at from another point of view than what is habitually done: one must look at it from the view of life. In doing so one could say: with reference to what has become available to the Proletariat as a result of what the ruling classes had to give him because they didn't want him to be left illiterate, through this the modern Proletarian had the desire to conquer, to take it as his inheritance what had been built up in the recent times out of the endeavours of the leading circles, what they had created as a scientific world view.

What it comes down to is this — now the modern Proletarian reacted in quite a different manner regarding this scientific world view than all the other circles, even though they were the ones who had created this world view. One could be quite an enlightened person in the leading and up to the-then ruling circles, a person whose innermost convictions welled up from the results of modern science, for my sake one could be a scientific researcher like *Vogt*, a popular scientific researcher like *Büchner*, and still your scientific orientation will be different to that of the modern Proletarian.

Those who, out of the leading circles with their prejudices, namely their anticipation and their presentiments, who theoretically confess to their modern education regarding human beings and nature, they remain stuck for this reason within a social order which cuts them off from the modern Proletariat. The structure of the Proletariat does not rest on scientific claims but is due to what came before modern science into human minds as religious, lawful and such imaginations towards the fulfilment of human dignity. Of this I once had a direct experience.

It happened in the moment when I stood in front of a worker gathering with the tragically passed away *Rosa Luxemburg*. We were addressing the gathering regarding the modern worker and modern science. There one could to see how, what modern science poured into the modern proletarian souls, worked quite differently even in the most convinced leading circles, when Rosa informed the people: 'There is nothing which refers to the angelic creation of people, nothing which points to the lofty places of origin which the common people eagerly describe; there are even claims from the common people's world view how our origins developed from climbing animals. Whoever thinks this through' — thus she spoke enthusiastically about this issue, this leader of the workers — 'whoever thinks this through can't discriminate like the present leading circles are doing, persisting in their prejudices about the possibilities of grading ranks among people who all originate from the same origins.' — This was taken up differently by them compared with those in the leading circles. This supplemented the ideas which the modern Proletarians were taken to understand as science.

That which has been taken up by a soul has the possibility for further development and about this evolution I would like to relate something to you.

If you glance over everything which relates to the question of how it is possible that the force of labour of the modern Proletarian has been made into goods, you will gradually be coerced through your observations regarding the economic life to arrive at a point where you have to say to yourself: It has come about precisely because the modern worker has been harnessed to the mere economic life and through being within this economic life his labour has become goods. In this direction, we have the continuation of the slave question of olden times. Here the entire person was goods. Today what has remained is only the labour of the person. However, now this power of labour must be adhered to by all people.

Within the modern Proletarian soul was the feeling that the last remnants from Barbarian times must not be allowed to continue into the future, that it should be conquered. There was no other way to conquer it than with the same clear strength of mind with which the modern Proletariat grasped the essence of economic- and human nature, with which the science for a healthy social organism can be grasped. About this science I would like to say a few words to you.

One thing above all appears clearly. One need to ask oneself: within the circulation of the modern economic life, what makes the force of labour of the modern Proletarian into goods? It is the economic power of the capitalists.

In these words of the power of the capitalists there is already an indication for a healthy answer. So: when is power diametrically opposed? Power is diametrically opposed by law, by rights. This however points out that for the healing, the recovery, of human labour in the social organism it can only come about when labour is taken out, when above all the question regarding labour is taken out of the economic process and it becomes a pure and clear question of law.

Through this we come to consider things in broader terms, whether there is a more significant difference between the economic question and the question of law. This distinction exists: only we are not inclined today to examine this difference deeply enough. We are not inclined to goo deeply enough into, on the one hand, what the active forces in all of economic life has to be, and on the other hand, what the active powers need to be in the actual life of rights.

What works in the economic processes? Human needs are active in the economic process; here the possibility of satisfying human needs may come through production. Both are based on natural foundations, the human requirements are based on people and production is based on climatic, geographic and such natural foundations. The economic life of the modern division of labour has led towards what the exchange of commodities is, and has to be. Each exchange of commodity which benefits both the needs of people and value of goods according to their mutual estimation — I can't describe it in detail, it would take too long

— appear on the markets and is drawn into the circulation of the economic process on the markets.

Within the circulation of the economic life, the life of the law can't develop simultaneously as a closed circuit. Human nature will as much admit that the social organism within the economic life develops the life of rights by itself, as it will admit that a single centralized system exists in the human organism. Tonight, I really don't want to play with various comparisons out of natural science but I believe here is the point which the natural scientist has also reached today, as we have done. In my last book "**Riddles of the Soul**" I have remarked that natural science can't properly acknowledge that there are three systems in the healthy human organism: the sense-nervous system is there as carrier of the soul life, the breathing and heart system as carrier of the rhythmic life and the metabolic system as carrier for metabolism and this comprises the entire human organism. However, each system is centralised in itself, each has its own approach to the outer world. In this human organism order and harmony is summoned in order for these three systems not to cause chaos among one another but that they unfold side by side, and as a result allow the power of one to flow into the other.

So in a healthy social organism such a three-foldness should take place. It must be realised that when a person in the economic organism becomes active, he must simply operate in the economic process. Then administration, the legislation of this economic process is expected to mutually evaluate the goods in the economic reality and bring it into movement towards a goal orientated circulation of goods, introducing the goods production, introducing the consumption of goods. What needs to be removed now from this economic process is not everything which includes the satisfaction of needs of one person to another, but is connected to the relationship of one person to every other person. Where all people should be equal is radically different from what can develop only in the economic life. That is why it is necessary for the healing of the social organism that the purely legal life element, the actual life of rights, be removed from the economic one. This development is just what has been striven against in recent times.

The ruling classes up to now — what have they done? In the regions where they felt comfortable, where their interests really lie, there you have the old merging which certainly had existed in many areas between the economic life and political state life, and now is taken further. So we see that in recent times, under the influence of the leading circles of mankind, so-called nationalisation came about in certain economic sectors. Post and telegraph and similar ones nationalised in a modern step which this modern progress wants.

In exactly the opposite direction it must be considered, not according to the interests of the leading circles up to now, but with the question: 'What are the foundations of a healthy social organism?' — Efforts need to be made to gradually dissolve the purely economic life from the actual political state, a state which has to care for law and order, but above all to care for those things that out of these areas, out of the economic life the corresponding life of law flows in. Those who have no eyes, no spiritual eyes, can't really distinguish how radically different the economic life is to the actual political state.

Look at how these things have developed today. Some people speak out of the present social conditions in such a way that they say, within the social conditions we have as the first item: 'Exchange goods for goods.' — Good, this happens in the economic life. It has just been spoken about. Now as to the second item: 'Exchange of goods, alternatively the representative of goods, namely money, for labour.' And as a third item: 'Exchange of goods for laws.'

What about this last one? I've just spoken about the second one. Now, we need to look at the relationship of property ownership within the modern economic order and we will immediately become clear about what should be clarified in this area for the future. How one usually likes to think about the ownership relationship in relation to land — everything else in the actual foregoing regarding the social organism doesn't really have meaning, the only meaning it has is that the owner of the ground and land has the right to own a piece of land and can utilise the earth, and by doing so make his personal interests valid.

This doesn't have the slightest relevance in the origins of the economic processes as such. With the economic processes — against this only an erroneous national economy objects — it relates to what there is on the land as goods or the value of goods that can be generated. Use of the land depends on a right.

This right, however, is turned into power, transformed within the modern capitalistic economic order, through the amalgamation of capitalism with land rental. So on the one side we have the power, excluded from such rights; on the other side economic power, which is able to compel human labour to become goods. From both sides, nothing other than the actualized white lie is the result, when there is no striving — striving out of actual social insight — towards the dividing of the social organism into an economic organism and an organism in the narrower sense, as state-political.

The economic organism must be established on an associative foundation, out of the needs of consumption in its relationship to production. Out of the various interests of the most varied career circles the manifold cooperatives — one could name them with the old word of 'brotherhood' — need to be developed, in which the needs and their fulfilment are managed.

What develops from this associative foundation of the economic organism will always relate to the fulfilment of one sphere of people with another sphere. In this area expert utilisation must be decisive, first in the natural foundations and then also in the design utilisation of the production, circulation and consumption of goods. What will be of relevance here would be human needs and human interests.

This is always regarded as contrary, as something radically different to how apparently equal people relate towards one another, where they should be equal; it is today already uttered in trivial words: 'Where they must stand equal before those laws which they have created themselves, as equals.'

On the associative foundation, the circulation of the economic process will rest; on a purely democratic basis, on the principle of equality of all people and their relationship to one another will rest, in a narrower sense, the actual political organisation. Out of this political organisation something quite different will develop compared to the economic power, which makes labour into goods. Out of the economic life, separated from the political life, something will rise as a true law of employment, where here and only here, the labour which can be traded between one person and another, measure, work and so on can be agreed upon.

However, one might believe that things in recent times have already improved a bit — but fundamentally it comes down to not having improved. By the way the Proletarians' labour is positioned in the economic process, the price of labour as goods and the price of other products are dependent on the value of the goods. Everyone can see this if one looks deeper into the economic process. It will be different if, independent of the laws of the economic life and its administration, out of the political state, out of the purely democratic administration and making of laws for the political state, a labour law can come into existence. What will happen then?

What will then happen is that a person, through his own labour, will stand through his particular relationship towards the social organism in an ever so lively a way, as we can see today in the foundations of nature. Within certain boundaries, such things as the technical fertility of the ground, and so on, can be shifted a bit; the fixed boundaries of the foundations of nature be shifted a bit; yet these natural foundations determine the economic life nevertheless in the most extensive measure from one side. Likewise, as the economic life is determined from this side, so from the other side the economic life must be determined from outside, so that it doesn't make labour dependent on it but that the economic life can be presented by purely human foundations. Then labour determines the price of goods, then goods don't determine the price of labour any longer!

At most it can happen that from some or other basis the power of labour can't manage sufficiently and the economic life is impoverished. The remedy should be sought in the correct basis and not merely in the economic life.

The basic economic life is only based on supply and demand. With labour rights, which is situated on the basis of an independent political state, all the rest of the rights are also necessarily based on this same foundation. Briefly — I can only indicate it due to our limited time — it must necessarily be seen how there has to be a peeling apart on both sides: the life of rights and the economic life, the ideal of a healthy social organism in the future.

As a third element, the independent economic life must be integrated with the independent law of rights, with what one can call the spiritual life on mankind.

By speaking of true progress within the Proletarian world view, one will encounter the most resistance. The opinion has come from thinking-habits in this sphere, more than elsewhere, that salvation depends on the absorption of the entire spiritual life by the state. People were unable to see through the dependence of their spiritual life coming from the state right now in recent times, from what had happened before in the so-called interests of the ruling state circles, which had been able to satisfy these ruling circles. These ruling circles discovered their interests were satisfied by the state; they allowed the state to absorb ever more, what they called the spiritual life. Like the political state necessitated obligatory tax laws and established that all people are equal before the law, and how it is necessary by the state, through the obligatory tax to satisfy its needs, so, on the other side the spiritual life had to be freed from both the other spheres of the social organism.

The striving towards the amalgamation of the spiritual life with the economic life has brought disaster into our recent times. That which is to develop in the spiritual life can only do so if it takes place in the light of true freedom. Everything which can't develop in the light of true freedom stunts and paralyses the real spiritual life and besides that, leads to going astray, which can be recognised all too easily in the newer social order. Of necessity, here is to figure out which inner connections exist between the spiritual life in the narrowest sense, and the religious life, the economic life, the artistic life, a certain ethical life — what the relationship is between the life of all of them which originates in the first place out of the individuality's abilities and skills.

Out of this now, while we are speaking about these things in the most serious way, when in the first instance a healthy social organism is considered, we must speak about it in such a way that the following needs are to be counted under the heading of spiritual life: everything which involves the unfolding and development of individual abilities, from the start of the schooling system through to the university system, right into the artistic, right into the ethical life, yes, right into those branches of the spiritual life which form the foundation of practical and even economic systems. In all these areas, the emancipation of the spiritual life is to be striven for. Thus, the spiritual life is to be placed as a free initiative of individual human capabilities, so that this free spiritual life can only be there in a corresponding way in a healthy social organism, when its validity also depends on free recognition, on the free understanding of those who need the acceptance. That means that in future the management of the spiritual life will no longer be directed out of an addition of sums of what there is in the purse or strongbox, nor come out of state bureaucracy.

Not only as a result of the spiritual life being governed by the state, did it take on a certain characteristic corresponding to the personalities within it, in relation to the personalities who administered it, but the spiritual life as we find it today, rightly experienced as an ideology by the modern proletariat, this spiritual life has actually become a mirror image of the interests and desires which the leading circles have for the modern state because this they created according to their own comforts and needs. Is it basically right to say that the entire spiritual life has gradually become only a mirrored superstructure for the economic and governmental life? The modern spiritual life of the leading circles is exactly such a superstructure. Certainly chemistry or mathematics can't easily take on characteristics according to the interests of the leading circles. Already within the scope in which they are practiced, especially the light which falls on them from other spiritual areas, is determined through the fact that the leading circles have interests in the modern state life and for the modern spiritual life to grow together with the state.

Yes, modern spiritual life is exactly at the most important stage where it should penetrate the human soul and take its particular position in the social order, but instead it has become a sporting ball of the economic and political life. One can see in the way in which, right into the terrible war catastrophes, the carriers of the spiritual life were connected to the modern state life through capitalistic detours, basically taking the most important spiritual areas of life and inserting what could be applied, to the service of the state.

Not a hundred, not a thousand but thousands of proofs can be found. You only need to think of taking *the* German history professors and supporters of historic science. Try to make an image of everything they have produced in relation to the history of the Hohenzollern, and ask yourself whether, according to this world historic fact, the history of the Hohenzollern actually looks like it does, as it had appeared before? According to this, one can observe how relationships within the spiritual life have become a mere game for those who were not liberated from it.

The spiritual life must become free from both other spheres. Only then can the spiritual life continue with its own legislation and administration — as strange and surprising as this might sound, but it needs to be said — of what today can only, and completely, come out of capitalistic prejudices; then spiritual life will really become the winner over purely economic proletarian interests. The spiritual life is consistent. The spiritual life comes out of the highest branch of spiritual life right down into those branches which originate as a result of someone, out of their individual talents, taking the lead in some or other venture. Just as he directs them today, so he directs them out of the economic life through the process of power, economic power. Like he leads them from out of a healthy social organism, so it comes out of the spiritual life. Spiritual life has within a healthy social organism its own legislation and administration in relation to the higher branch of spiritual life, but also in relation to everything within the economic process which work towards the spiritual life being independent as such.

Then within this economic process the right way and influences of emancipation will rise towards an independent spiritual life. What had been achieved through capital can no longer be achieved according to the sense of modern capitalism. Now it will be achieved only through the impulses coming out of the spiritual life itself.

However, these impulses must be imagined in the correct way. How will an enterprise really look in line with these impulses?

Whoever knows the foundations of spiritual life — I have come across this quite often — will not contradict me when I give the following sketch of an enterprise which obtained its impulses not from an economic influence but from a spiritual power. Here would be those who are in the position, out of a free understanding with their colleagues and with a certain capital fund, to undertake nothing related to their own needs but directed to a social understanding which has been truly founded in spiritual life. In such an enterprise they would face, through a free understanding of all colleagues, right down to the last worker, the free understanding of their appointed posts, then a relationship of free understanding will arise between the leaders of the enterprise and the workers who are quite necessary for its execution. This results in, that beside the working hours there is included, within this enterprise and within the cooperatives of the enterprise, the possibility of a free expression about the entire way in which the overall social organism is placed within the economic process. Then those who live within the influences of a spiritual life would replace those in positions held by capitalist entrepreneurs today and reveal themselves in regard to all which places their wares in the entire social process of mankind. Each individual will then see the direction taken by the product to which they have contributed their work, where the product of their particular individual capabilities of manual work leads to. Everything can then also become included which would give the worker the possibilities to establish a real employment contract.

A real employment contract can't be determined when it is established on the basis of the condition that labour is goods. A true employment contract must not be based along these lines: the one and only real employment contract can only be based on the condition that work, which is necessary for the creation of products, is accomplished on the basis of laws, but that in relation to economics, that the proper cooperation is created between manual work and spiritual work, that in relation to economics, that a sharing operation between the manual and spiritual work must happen which can only take place out of the free understanding that manual work was the precursor, because then the manual worker knows that out of the spiritual coexistence with the leaders to what degree his work, through their leadership, flows for his own benefit into the social organism.

In such collaboration, the possibility ceases for capital based enterprises to develop according to egotistic benefits. Then only, when in this way the social organism is healed, then only can today's profit motives be replaced by purely factual interest. To a greater extent what had been the case in earlier times, would arise again as the interconnection between a person and his or her work.

Let us consider the connection between a person and their work today. On the one hand, there is the entrepreneur who wants to accomplish what he regards as work but he clears off as quickly as possible from this work. He expresses it in such a way that when he has cleared out from his work, he refers to it as "shoptalk." He gets away from it and then searches through all kinds of other things to discover his striving as a human being. Through this relationship of human beings to their work is shown how little people grow together with their work.

This is an unhealthy relationship. This unhealthy relationship attracts others; by this tearing the modern Proletariat away from the foundation of their old craft, where they grew with their occupation, grew from their professions to their honour, to their human dignity, tear them away to where they are installed at machines, harnessed in a factory; here the unhealthy proof is produced in them that they can obtain no relationship with their jobs.

Whoever has come to know the true foundations of spiritual life knows that such an unhealthy relationship between a person and his occupation can only arise from unhealthy requirements. There is nothing in a healthy spiritual life which is free from political and free from the economic life which only have an effect on them; there is nothing in such a spiritual life which is not directly interesting and which, when it is correctly handled, a person can connect to his work, because he knows: this work he does, becomes a member of the circulation of the social organism. It is not something which can only be judged because it can't be any other way, that a person must also do something uninteresting. No, it must bc judgcd in such a manner that precisely this foundation of spiritual life will be searched for, which is the one and only thing which can call forth interest: coherence of people with their work and interest in all spheres in any occupation.

This will show that, when the emancipated free spiritual life out of spiritual impulses enter right into the most individualised branches of governmental and economic life and its administrators, then only will it be possible that a real, factual interest is applied to all and not be based on a mere commercial, mere outer economic and benefit ratio relationship.

Admittedly the foundations for such a spiritual life need to be created. These foundations can only be created when everything regarding schooling is to be placed in the management of the spiritual life, when the lowest teacher no longer asks: what does the political state expect of me? — but when he or she can look at those in whom they have trust, when he or she can look at the spiritual life according to their own principles in their managed area of the social organism.

Thus, it works in many respects, I believe, when it proves itself naturally. From a true continuation of the proletarian world viewpoint it works against habits of thought. While people had absorbed the inheritance of the bourgeois science and amalgamated spiritual life, state and economic life into one another, it is important that for the healing of the social organism there needs to be a striving towards the independence of these three mentioned areas. Only through these areas

— if I might use acceptable expressions — gradually having their own parliament and their own management, which relate to one another like a government of a sovereign state, only negotiating through delegation, only exchanging their communal needs through transport, then only will the social organism be healed. The question today is a fundamental one, arising out of all the facts: How can the social organism be healed? It needs to be taken in hand, it is sick, this social organism!

In order for those who, out of their class consciousness, want to make the correct claim towards healing the social organism, they actually need to research the Proletarian world viewpoint down to its fertile sprout and from there continue to build further.

I must admit that initially some could object to what is considered as correct today, when it is said: The direction must be taken according to this social three-foldness, this three-foldness of the social organism. — As much as these ideas contradict thought habits of some people at present, the reality must not be to steer towards our comforts, not towards what we believe has up to now been true for life practitioners. Reality needs to orientate us, reality founded on honesty and a healthy sense of judgment for the recognition of truth.

What I have explored here has no relevance to some or other cloud-cuckoo land. Oh, the time is here when some, who can only glance superficially at the simplest things and then create their own thought patterns, considering themselves practical in life, must admit that the very frowned-upon idealists who think from the basis of evolutionary necessities of mankind, are the real practical people. What I have given you is not clouds of cuckoo land; it originated exactly out of the most direct, daily needs in the life of mankind.

Admittedly I can't enter into all the single areas; in conclusion, I would like to touch on one area, an area which I can only mention fleetingly as something which I've apparently derived from the most ancient idea of the social life and how it comes across as the most ardent need. What in life is most humiliating? The most humiliating thing is that we must have what we call money, in our purse. We also know however, what is connected to this money. You know how this money intervenes into every part of life. If one considers the development of a healthy social organism, in which branch does the control of money belong?

The management of money has up to now been the concern of the state through certain forces of its development. Money is actually truly goods in a healthy organism, just as labour is not goods. Everything unhealthy which comes through how money enters the social organism results from money being stripped of its characteristic as goods, that it depends today more on the cancellation of some market through the political state, than on what it certainly should rest, while nothing else works in international traffic, which is on its merchandise value. National economists have an amusing battle today, a battle which really works in an amusing way to the insightful. They ask if money is goods, just a popular commodity, for which one can always swap other goods, whereas if for instance you had the misfortune of only manufacturing tables and chairs, you would have to go around dragging your tables and chairs and wait for someone who had vegetables. Instead you could swap your tables and chairs for the money they are worth and then find what's applicable according to your needs. While the one says money is a commodity or at least represents a commodity, even if it is paper money, for which there is a corresponding value, the other might say money is totally only that which comes about through the state law pigeon-holing a certain brand. Now these educated economists research the question: What is correct? Is money a commodity or something which arises from mere branding? Is it a mere payment for goods?

The answer is simply this: today money is neither the one nor the other, but both. The one is a result of the state simply approving of certain brands; the other is that in international transportation or in a certain relation also in national transportation, money purely as a commodity is the only form in which it can participate in the circulation.

A healthy social organism will strip money of its legal characteristics; its management and legislation will be assigned through a natural process within itself, in the adjustment of money, coinage, the value of money within the economic circulation, the same parliament, the same organisation which manages the rest of the economic organism.

Only then, when something like this steps in, which the modern Proletariat may be striving for, will it be placed on a healthy foundation. That strange relationship which exists between the working wages and the nature of goods, this relationship depends on a white lie. While the worker on the one hand believes that when his demand for an increased wage will suffice towards healthier living conditions, then on the other hand the price of commodities rises if it is not freed in the economic cycle from the legal cycle of the political state. These things are all placed on a healthy foundation only when the three-foldness steps in.

In the same way, if you have insight into the necessity of independence of the spiritual life, then you will see, will accept that there is no necessity to create capitalistic organisations as such, but that the manner and way how in the course of modern time capital is managed, how it has been used, that it only exists in the economic process, is how the capital process has caused damage which is linked to so much misery.

One will have to recognise this: as long as the employment contract does not relate to the collective output of what the crafter and the spiritual worker brings, but as long as the employment contract is related to the wages for the work, for so long would it be impossible to place these on a healthy basis.

The one and only way for the spiritual life to be recognised as a healthy reality becomes revealed in any case in its necessary relationship between worker and spiritual ruler, there where the worker is cheated, not cheated merely through the economy but cheated by the business man, who does not value his individual qualities, his spiritual traits in the right way, but in an incorrect way, in a inhuman manner. The worker is not exploited by the economic life, the worker is exploited through the white lies which come about in today's social organism in which individual abilities can just be used by cheating the workers because they are not seen from both sides in the economic process; within a healthy spiritual life they are seen from both sides and directed thus.

As I've said, what I've brought here towards the healing of the social organism can still be resisted by many Proletarian minds. I can see this. For years I have been involved with workers and spoken to them about these things. I haven't managed only single branches of teaching in the workers educational school; I have also offered exercises in speech. In these exercises which led on to speech exercises, several workers in this community truly showed what particular colouring, what special form their demands took as modern Proletariat. Here one could readily acquire the ability to think about the Proletariat not only in the manner of today's leading circles or the leading circles up to now. This is what I wanted to say to you today: think with the Proletariat, don't think about them!

For my sake think about it, it is like this — I would like to bring you to understand — that with reference to the contents of the one or the other meaning, one could perhaps renounce one but it is not important in today's world historic time whether one denies one or other meaning but that one agrees as to their honest claims which should be the claims of the modern Proletariat. Only through becoming comfortable with these agreements, with the consensus of honest *Willing*, then only through this could the seedling be discovered, which lies in the Proletarian world view, towards further growth and development. The time for mere discussion is over, the time is past for people who only want to serve their interests and speak about understanding. The time has come where for decades already, merely the undercurrents of outstanding claims of the modern Proletarians have now stepped up to the world historic plan, where they may really become the most important and most meaningful events in modern times.

What has come out of the chaos of the recent world war due to the economic war, which for a long time might in future continue to meet the future, this will become the social question. Today I will present no unreal, no theoretical solution or attempt to give one. I want to make you aware that the time has now come for the social question to present itself, where people in their social communal work need to be divided into governmental-, economic- and spiritual organs, that out of these healthy divisions a continued solution of the social question can come about.

This social question will not be solved from one day to the next once it is there; because it will always be there like life always generates new conflicts, so there needs to be this branching of members which strives in an honest way for solutions in the rising conflicts in social life. Whether people would try, in the widest circles, to become aware of such an evolution in the proletarian world view for the healing which would lie in the future, would depend on the direction taken from the starting point of the modern proletarian movement. Actually, it needs to lead to something which has not been able to come about yet. Out of all the eligible demands of the questions of wages, of bread, it needs to be lifted up to a mighty, radical world historic change, coming out of the consciousness of the modern worker and passing over into general human consciousness, out of the dignity, out of the sensitive dignity of the modern Proletarian, to be established as real dignity for all people.

In the attached discussion, various speakers were heard and the conclusion was given in the following words by Rudolf Steiner:

Rudolf Steiner: Yes, regarding the first honourable speaker I would like to make something like a fundamental remark. When one speaks one is often in the position to say that one can't quite grasp why things which the previous speaker uttered are not quite understandable, as if it had been said as a refutation of what one had just said. The first speaker spoke in such a way as if he found it necessary to assure me in every way — even though he has acknowledged many things, at least in relation to his whole attitude — that he actually has to fight. I'm not in a position to fight with him but I would like to say that actually those who have listened to me don't have so much against what the first speaker had said. I am in the position to acknowledge much more, also in relation to the content of his statements, than what he somehow seemed to focus on in relation to what I actually wanted.

Now, some details seem important. It is remarkable that the first speaker believes that according to my lecture I spoke to workers, but I did not work with them. Sure, naturally each one can only work in his area of expertise, but the manner and way in which I worked together with the workers is already such that one can't say: 'the workers were merely spoken to.' I also believe that those who perhaps enter more into what streams through the lecture, on its entire intention, will find it understandable that for so many years I have not been addressed in this way, even though I admit I have been thus addressed today. I have not always been addressed like this, only I believe, out of the simple reason that at that time workers already felt that what I had to say was not uttered from mere conversations with workers.

When it became possible for me to speak in such a way as I have had to do today, it is really not some learned skill. Let us pose the question: Who can actually implicate themselves as Proletarians? Whoever can speak with and to the Proletarian about his destiny which he has struggled through with his own forces, can speak in such a way as I have done today, only as a free speaker. In these circles I have been accused, shared community, I have perhaps even been treated nearly, perhaps even treated worse, than I've been handled here this evening. Surely it is something different when someone, like me, has struggled through in a similar way; I will continue thus in my short life which remains. I have struggled for years through conversations with the Proletarians, worked with the Proletarians, I have grown out of the Proletariat, grown hungry with the Proletarians. I didn't ask the Postman how much he earns to make him starve, but I had to become hungry myself. I didn't get to understand the Proletarians through thinking about them but I learnt to understand the Proletarians by living with them. I grew up out of the Proletariat, learned to starve because I had to starve. This is the foundation from which you can already sense that because I've been able to live for years with them, I don't speak as it it's a mere theory but from a position of an applicable practical position. I believe it can also give the basis whether one has a certain right to speak to the Proletarians or not.

This is what I wanted to say about this issue.

What the first speaker brought, for the greatest part, doesn't actually relate to me but to the intellectuals. Yes, the chairman has since said: 'When someone or other can speak about being pelted with dirt, dirt thrown at him by the intellectuals, then I may do it too.' Really, when you want to investigate the manner and way in which dirt has been thrown at me, and the way and manner this dirt looks like, then you will not envy the dealings I have entertained with the intellectuals.

Anyway, this is a personal remark. However, those who have replied to me, also come from a personal basis and therefore these remarks need to be made.

Now, the greatest part of course doesn't involve me but it has relevance to the student body. In relation to the latter: do you believe that I don't understand at all how the majority of today's student body is justified by the reproach that this ideal does not reach the lowest wage-labourer? Obviously here much can be argued regarding capital. Just as the modern worker, on the other hand, understands that after all, other classes of people have developed out of circumstances, so eventually the modern student has also had to develop out of their situation. Whoever can impartially compare the strivings within the modern student body with for instance what was found within the student body, when I also — it's been a while — had been within that student body, it was said, in reference to the profundity in just the phenomena of decline in the bourgeoisie, as contained in the modern professorial body — which obviously depends on the student body — that in relation to the example which illuminated the modern student body one can above all observe the blossoming which brings improvements to the students, which in itself has a certain satisfaction. It has become quite obvious — when today it looks as if the students would stick the workers in the back — that out of the colleagues of the student body, I believe there are quite large numbers already, it will rise towards social ideals. The student has to overcome various things. One must not forget how unshakable the clamps are which immobilises one. I have just recently had many an opportunity to also speak to young students, whose ideals appear unreachable to them yet they are closer to having developed a healthy spiritual life in general out of the sick spiritual life of today. I know what kind of receptivity the youth has for the renewal of the spiritual life. I know also, however, how great the temptation is, when inspired youth who have graduated, who find it necessary to search for a position in the modern community, how close the temptation lies to become dulled and fall back into the infidelity of philistinism.

Naturally we won't reach a final solution from one day to the next for what we most hope and wish to see. However, it must be acknowledged that everywhere where such a longing exists, this kind of sensible yearning which the modern Proletariat calls for, takes place, that it isn't suppressed and in some fanatic or dogmatic way mixed with one another. I still believe that this dogmatism at least up to a certain degree — even in modern struggles the funds can't be too easily chosen — would have to yield to the spirit which I've presented in my lectures: what is important is not so much the variety of thoughts but more on the equality of earnest will forces.

Just ask for once how many of those you blame for sticking one in the back are dependent on the circumstances established by the modern student, and ask yourself on the other hand, how much earnest will is valid in today's youth. Rather maintain that, than falling into dogmatism and becoming lamed.

Now, what I can say about the content brought by the second speaker is this: I agree to the call which has fallen to the left, which is basically not so very different from what I said myself: I don't claim things need to be as firmly said as I've expressed them. When something or other is said which can improve things, then I'm pleased about it. As a result, I don't judge as harshly as the second speaker has done; I would only like to put right what can always be referred to by this speaker who has not quite taken it in a right way. He has for instance referred with suspicion to the worker school where I taught for many years in Berlin by saying it could only be a liberal educational association. I have clearly stressed that it came from the old Liebknecht, the labour school was founded by Wilhelm Liebknecht! I don't believe you can push over the old Liebknecht with founding an arbitrary educational association for the working class as they would not have accepted him at the time. The audience wasn't made up out of the "ordinary bourgeois liberals" but were entirely comprised of workers who were none other than social democrats out of Proletarian circles organised through the bank!

So I believe that some of the words I have spoken have not been taken up in the right way by this speaker, as I would have liked them to be taken, and how they can be understood when not approached with a predetermined opinion when the other person arrives with a different meaning, but when he expresses what is meant only in a different form because he believes it is necessary that this world historic moment must be taken more comprehensively, and while he believes that today not every practical person can be called who would only judge in relation to the near future but a true practical person who overviews the bigger picture.

In relation to the question of the "call for proposals," which corresponds nearly word-for-word to what I've said tonight — you need not wonder about it because you have heard that the "call" was created by me and that you need not expect that when I speak about something to the bourgeoisie, that it should sound different to when I speak here from this podium.

Interruption: Either everywhere the same or...

That's what I've just said. I said in the "call" are the same words as what I've said here. In every "call" there is nothing different to what I've said here.

For me it is important that the meaning of what I say is the truth and I will speak the truth in every instance where I am permitted to speak the truth. I only speak the truth; that is what it comes down to, for me. This is what I want to say in relation to this. I will exclude no one from anything if he can merge it with his conviction and can say yes to what I say myself. I believe this is the only way to arrive at an olive branch, that we speak the truth, unconcerned about the impression made on people, whether they support it or not. This is what I wanted to say about this.

In conclusion, I would like to make a remark which relates to what the next speaker said: I had not said anything about the manner of the struggle. — However, out of my words you can extract how I actually think about this struggle. I believe I've referred to it sufficiently; my view does not depend on a superficial understanding or how the nice things are all mentioned. Today we are enslaved in a facts-phase where our deeds are nothing but an empty observation of how things must be changed, however we need, through our observation, to find which new thoughts are really able to be brought into human souls. The ancient thoughts showed what kind of a social order they could bring about and these old thoughts are the proof that they are useless. For this reason, I believe that it first and foremost practically comes down to those who have an honest social will, to communicate before anything else about what can happen.

Today we stand here in Switzerland — I don't know if one could say "Thanks to God" or "unfortunately" — still in the circumstances which are not the same as in the central and eastern European circumstances. Central and eastern Europe is in circumstances only manageable through the connection to the ancient thinking of a social organism. When there is no effort made by the Proletariat themselves to utter the fundamental questions, which now out of this chaos through the simplest organisations, which all have to have the characteristics, according to my view, of this three-foldness of the social organism — if healing is not brought about by the Proletariat themselves, by organisations being newly recreated, according to new ideas, then I see absolutely no healing in the coming decades.

First of all, we need to begin with something you might regard as insignificant: we must realize we don't only face civil institutions, bourgeois conditions but that we face a bourgeois science.

This is what I've said in the Berlin union house for sixteen years and it was really understood among the Proletarians. The Proletariat still have the task of expelling thoughts of bourgeois science out of their thinking and not to meet some or other institutions with the bourgeois science but with new thoughts, which perhaps can only be brought by the Proletariat because the Proletariat are emancipated from all the remaining human relationship in which unfortunately the bourgeois people stand. Today the most important thing is something which probably appears as the least important to you, the emancipation of spiritual life; the accomplishment of the development of freedom of the spiritual life. If we accomplish in having a free spiritual life, if we manage to have a science which is not a mere capitalist tributary and thus indicate this tone into the Proletarian circles, then only can we approach healing. Not a restriction in the bourgeois sense, not a reduction but rather an amplification of proletarian activities.

I have the firm belief — if people were capable of arguing like the second speaker from a viewpoint which I well understand, and apply so many objections that one can't understand, sentence by sentence, what I've said — I have the firm belief, because I have spent much of life among the Proletariat, that what I have said is understood not from other classes but would be understood by the Proletariat. Unfortunately, we have to wait until the Proletariat understand it. I do believe however that it will be understood.

With these thoughts, I would like to say, I can with a certain satisfaction look back at what I've wanted to achieve this evening. I really haven't wanted to convince you right into the details of every word. I am taking into consideration your free individualities; to each one of you I take care to allow for your understanding, out of freedom.

I do believe that among you there are many who will still think differently about what I have said, as you already thought about it today. This belief is the very thing which needs to be applied to healing the social organism.

COVER ARTWORK

Title:	**Community Life**
Artist:	**Hanna von Maltitz**
Year:	**2011**
Material:	**Oil on canvas board**
Dimensions:	**50 x 70 cm**
Where:	**Artist's Collection**
Notes:	**Price: ZAR 3,000**

THE FUTURE OF ANTHROPOSOPHICAL PUBLICATIONS

The Internet is about choice, and choice means the freedom to choose. The *Rudolf Steiner Archive & e.Lib* believes this is what the future of publications — the dissemination of knowledge — is all about.

This publication absolutely falls in that category: the freedom to choose whether to just use the information we present on-line, or use that information and purchase one of our other offerings, like a hardcopy of the book, or a softcopy version, like a CD or something for your Kindle. Proceeds from your purchases help us to continue these efforts to bring newly translated material to researchers and Rudolf Steiner aficionados all over the world. Freedom is a gift ... it is a gift of love. And as John Lennon wrote, "Love is all there is!"

RELATED MATERIAL

Rudolf Steiner on Social Issues:

www.rsarchive.org/SocialIssues/index.php

The Social Issues Section of the Rudolf Steiner Archive presents some of the lectures and publications of Rudolf Steiner that are related to Social Issues. In the Catalogue of Holdings, the works are categorized as lectures, articles, books, etc. Works presented here may be accessed from the Catalogue, from our Main Steiner Archive Menu, or by selecting a subject area from the Sections list at the upper left of this page.

Basic Issues of the Social Question:

wn.rsarchive.org/Lectures/GA023/English/SCR2001/GA023_index.html

This book was written in 1919, just after the First World War, and suggests solutions to the social, political and economic problems of those times. At the end of the book, Steiner writes: "... either people will accommodate their thinking to the requirements of reality, or they will have learned nothing from the calamity and will cause innumerable new ones to occur in the future." History since then has proven these words to be prophetic. The "social question" has not been resolved, nor have steps been taken to initiate the healing process. We all too often look to the political state for the solutions to all social problems, be they of an economic, cultural or political nature. Steiner's concept of a tripartite, or threefold society in which the economic, cultural and political spheres would enjoy relative autonomy within the social organism has not yet been tried. This book contains his basic ideas for the restructuring of society.

The Renewal of the Social Organism:

wn.rsarchive.org/Lectures/GA024/English/AP1985/GA024_index.html

The articles presented in this volume were written during 1919 and 1920. In the Collected Edition of Rudolf Steiner's works, the volume containing the German texts is entitled, Aufsätze über die Dreigliederung des sozialen Organismus und zur Zeitlage 1915-1921 (Vol. 24 in the Bibliographic Survey, 1961.). They were translated from the German by E. Bowen-Wedgewood and Ruth Mariott; the translation was revised by Frederick Amrine. The publication of the printed volume was made possible by a grant from the Dietrich V. Asten Memorial Fund.

The Inner Aspect of the Social Question:

wn.rsarchive.org/Lectures/GA193/English/RSP1974/InnAsp_index.html

Rudolf Steiner suggested new ways to organize society and engage with social questions. This book presents his esoteric perspective on such concerns. Steiner asserts that we must begin by giving real value to the human element in the world, finding a deeper understanding of our relationship to nature and to the cosmos. Accordingly, it is ineffective to organize society in an arbitrary way; society ought to reflect the human relationship to the spiritual world. Steiner goes on to discuss the threefold archetype of social life — the political state, the economy, and the spiritual and cultural aspects — and how these three areas can interact in a healthy way, leading to an evolving society that is vibrant.

The Riddles of the Soul:

www.rsarchive.org/Books/GA021/index.php

The title, Riddles of the Soul. Anthropology and anthroposophy, Max Dessoir about anthroposophy, Franz Brentano (an obituary). Sketchy extensions, says a lot. The statements in this publication that Rudolf Steiner pulls "some of the scientific threads that need to be drawn from the philosophy of anthroposophy, the psychology and physiology." The significant finding of tripartism of the human organism finds its first representation here.

The Philosophy of Freedom/Spiritual Activity:

www.rsarchive.org/Books/GA004/index.php

This book, written in 1894, is a fundamental treatment of Steiner's philosophical outlook. Together with *Truth and Science* and *The Riddles of Philosophy* it might be considered as one third of a philosophical trilogy. The emphasis of the book is not on "freedom" as ordinarily understood, but is on "freiheit" or what might be termed freeness, or freehood. This freeness is a self-starting, self-directing activity of a spiritual sort. Here, the term "spiritual" is used in a sense not incompatible with the use of the word in the tradition of the German idealistic school of philosophy. It was originally published in German as, Die Philosophie der Freiheit. Grundzüge einer modernen Weltanschauung. Seelische Beobachtungsrelultate nach naturwissenschaftlicher Methode.

52245011R00100

Made in the USA
Middletown, DE
17 November 2017